Herman
A Wilderness Saint

T0293930

Herman
A Wilderness Saint

From Sarov, Russia to Kodiak, Alaska

Sergei Korsun with Lydia Black

Translated by Priest Daniel Marshall

Holy Trinity Publications
The Printshop of St Job of Pochaev
Holy Trinity Monastery
Jordanville, New York
2012

Herman, A Wilderness Saint
Copyright © 2012 Holy Trinity Monastery

HOLY TRINITY PUBLICATIONS
The Printshop of St Job of Pochaev
Holy Trinity Monastery
Jordanville, New York 13361-0036
www.holytrinitypublications.com

Translated from
Преподобный Герман Аляскинский, валаамский подвижник в Америке:
Материалы к жизнеописанию
Автор-составитель С.А. Корсунъ
Валаамский монастырь, Санкт-Петербург, 2005
ISBN 5-94263-007-0
and
Преподобный Германъ Аляскинскій: Жизнеописаніе,
Holy Trinity Monastery, Jordanville, NY, 2002
Составитель Сергій Корсунъ
ISBN 0-88465-071-5

ISBN: 978-0-88465-192-5 (paperback)
ISBN: 978-0-88465-205-2 (ePub)
ISBN: 978-0-88465-304-2 (Mobipocket)
Library of Congress Control 2010940794

CONTENTS

Icon of St Herman,
the work of Hieromonk Andrei (Erastov),
Jordanville, N.Y.

FOREWORD TO THE ENGLISH-LANGUAGE EDITION

St Herman of Alaska is one of the most widely venerated of saints by the Orthodox Christian people of North America, with churches and monasteries being dedicated to his memory. During his lifetime, he was known as a defender of the native Alaskan peoples from the rapacious practices of many of his fellow Russians whose interest in Alaska was commercial rather than Christian.

This book is not written in a hagiographical style but as history understood within the context of an Orthodox worldview. It contains materials not previously published in English and drawn from sources that were not accessible to scholars during the Communist period of the twentieth century. As such it offers a more comprehensive picture of the saint than has been seen before. Particularly fascinating is his connection to St Seraphim of Sarov, another Russian saint canonized in the twentieth century, and perhaps the best known modern Orthodox saint in the world.

Primary sources are used throughout the text in such a way that the reader will come to see St Herman and the key events that shaped his life through the eyes of his contemporaries, both friend and foe. These sources are carefully analyzed and compared to others in an effort to draw out the most accurate portrayal of events. Thus, the work will be of interest not only to those who already know and love the saint, but also to students of Russian-American history and the ethnology of the native peoples of Alaska.

As indicated by the table of contents, the main body of the work introduces us to St Herman during his lifetime, followed by appendixes that describe how devotion to him grew after his repose in 1836 and how his monastic labors have been continued by others up to our own time, culminating in his canonization in 1970. May we continue to be inspired by his life and aided by his prayers as we seek to live lives faithful to the Gospel of Christ wherever God has placed us.

Jordanville, 2012

INTRODUCTION

The biography of St Herman of Alaska was compiled by the brotherhood of Valaam Monastery and first published in 1868 under the title *The Life of the Valaam Monk Herman: An American Missionary*.[1] A second edition with insignificant changes came out in 1894. The first edition of Valaam Ascetics[2] was published in 1872, followed by a second edition in 1891 and a third edition in 1997. This work also included the biography of St Herman of Alaska.

In 1894, in honor of the centennial of the Kodiak Orthodox mission, the Valaam Monastery press published *Studies in the History of the American Orthodox Spiritual Mission (Kodiak Mission 1794–1837)*.[3] In 1900, a second edition of this book came out under the new title *Valaam Missionaries in America (at the End of the Eighteenth Century)*.[4] The biography of St Herman appears in a more expanded form in this book.

The sources for this life of St Herman of Alaska were the aforementioned books as well as several other publications. The intent is to give the reader an opportunity to get a sense of the historical situation and the specific conditions under which St Herman labored as a missionary. Both he and the other members of the mission were subject to continual persecution by local authorities—"the strong of this world." Why were they persecuted? Primarily because the missionaries wanted to live by the commandments of Christianity, and they called on their flock to do so as well. Documents attesting to this assume the leading role in this book.

Several dates in the life of St Herman about which biographers and historians hold varying opinions deserve special mention. There are two accounts of St Herman's entry into monasticism. According to Simeon Ivanovich Ianovskii's[5] letter of January 22, 1865, to the abbot of Valaam Monastery, St Herman was from the city of Serpukhov, became a novice of Holy Trinity–St Sergius Hermitage near St Petersburg when he was sixteen, and then moved to Valaam Monastery. This account was accepted by the Valaam Monastery brotherhood when they composed the biography of St Herman in 1867. This account is, however, in error because Ianovskii mixed up St Herman's biographical details with those of the monk Joseph, both of whom he met in Alaska in 1819. It is actually Father Joseph who was from Serpukhov and who became a novice at a very young age.

According to Ferdinand Peterovich Wrangell, St Herman left Sarov Monastery at the age of seventeen: "This esteemed man is among the most remarkable of people. A native of the Voronezh province,[6] he was from a (peasant) family of not wealthy, but prosperous parents. Having been picked as a [military] recruit, yet being driven from within to a different kind of life, he secretly left home at the age of seventeen and became a monk in a nearby monastery, Sarov."[7] Subsequently, he and a few others moved from Sarov to Valaam Monastery.[8] Archimandrite Feofan (Sokolov) mentions that St Herman was at Sarov Monastery in his youth. Additionally, in one of his letters, St Herman mentions an elder Joachim from Sarov Monastery with whom he was well acquainted. Therefore, three pieces of evidence confirm that St Herman laid the foundation for his monastic life in Sarov Monastery.

St Herman could have moved to Valaam Monastery no earlier than 1782. This is the year that Father Nazarius and four novices arrived at Valaam from Sarov Monastery.[9] One of them was soon tonsured a monk with the name Herman. This novice, Egor Ivanovich Popov, was tonsured November 1, 1782, at the age of thirty-one. Popov was accepted as a novice at Sarov Monastery in 1778, having been discharged because of illness in the previous year from the position of junior clerk in the military command of Kadom, a city in the Shatskoi district of the Voronezh province. There is no record of when and how Popov began his service in the office of the military command. Most likely, Popov had drawn the lot to be drafted but left for Sarov Monastery, as Wrangell mentioned, and was taken into the military from there.

The literary talent evident in his letters is circumstantial confirmation of the fact that Popov was the future St Herman. It was not an accident that he served as an assistant to the clerk: in the eighteenth century, there were few literate peasants, and only a few of those could write elegantly. It should be noted that while serving in Alaska, St Herman had a large library of religious books.[10] Moreover, this account is also supported by the fact that in the eighteenth century, novices at Valaam Monastery were not tonsured monks before age thirty.[11] All the members of the Kodiak mission who became monks at Valaam Monastery were tonsured when they were at least thirty years old: Hieromonk Juvenaly at age thirty-two, Hieromonk Athanasius at thirty, Hierodeacon Nectarios at thirty, and monk Herman in 1783 at thirty-one.

Documentary evidence of St Herman's date of birth is contradictory. The Book of Records in Holy Resurrection Church on Kodiak Island stated that he reposed in 1836 in his seventy-sixth year, meaning that he was born in 1760. In 1805, Father Gideon, inspector of the Kodiak mission, wrote in a letter that Father Herman was 48, indicating that he was born in 1757 (although this letter also incorrectly states Hierodeacon Nectarios's date of birth). If the novice Egor Popov was the future St Herman, then his birth year was 1751.

Thus, by tying together the fragmentary evidence of St Herman's youth, it is most logical to conclude that Egor

Ivanovich Popov, who became a monk at Valaam Monastery in 1782, was indeed the future enlightener of the Kodiak Aleuts, Venerable Herman of Alaska. He became a novice in Sarov Monastery in 1778, the very same year as Prokhor Moshnin, the future St Seraphim, Wonder-Worker of Sarov.

The time of St Herman's move to Spruce Island has likewise not been established. It can be presumed that this move occurred sometime between 1811 and 1817, although certainly not later than 1817.

Evidence about the date of St Herman's repose is also contradictory. Various sources give three dates: November 15, 1836; December 13, 1836; and December 13, 1837. The last date is clearly incorrect and has been discarded by the majority of experts. December 13, 1836, is written in the Book of Records at Holy Resurrection Church on Kodiak Island, but this is the date of his burial, not the date of his repose. This fact is confirmed by oral tradition on Kodiak, which holds that St Herman was buried a month after his repose. The most likely date of his repose is November 15, 1836. This is the date given for the repose of St Herman in a dispatch from the Russian Colonial Chief Manager Ivan A. Kupreianov to the main office of the Russian-American Company (RAC) in St Petersburg.

A few other details concerning other members of the Kodiak Orthodox mission have also been clarified. Several publications, for instance, maintained that Father Nectarios died in 1814 in Kirenskii Monastery and that Father Athanasius returned to Russia, to Valaam, and died there in 1825. The true date of Father Nectarios's death is 1831, as mentioned in *Valaam Monastery and Its Ascetics*.[12] Using archival evidence of the Most-Holy Synod, the vice chairman of the Society for the Religious and Moral Enlightenment of the Orthodox Church,[13] Apollinarii Nikolaevich L'vov, established that Father Nectarios died in Valaam Monastery in 1808.

The preeminent historian of Russian America, Lydia Sergeevna Black, a resident of Kodiak Island where St Herman's relics lie, provided letters from Kupreianov and Matvei Ivanovich Murav'ev and composed Appendix 1 to this work.

A number of the documents included here are published for the first time. Letters from the archives of Holy Resurrection Church on Kodiak Island that have been included were published more than 100 years ago in the magazine *American Orthodox Messenger*[14] and have rarely been used by researchers.

Although the documentary evidence regarding the life of St Herman of Alaska, Enlightener of America, is relatively small, his memory has been preserved in the hearts of his flock, the mostly illiterate Kodiak Aleuts; it is largely thanks to them that it has been preserved to this day. For this, as in all things, thanks be to the Lord!

Sergei A. Korsun, PhD, History
St Petersburg, Russia, 2005

CHAPTER I

St Herman's Call:
From Sarov to Valaam Monastery

St Herman of Alaska's biography should begin with Ferdinand Peterovich Wrangell's evidence that identifies St Herman as Egor Ivanovich Popov.[15] He was born in 1751 in a village of the Voronezh province to a very pious peasant family. It is known that one of his relatives finished her days as a nun of the famous Strastnoi Monastery in Moscow.

From his early childhood, the young Egor possessed a great zeal for piety; he went on many pilgrimages to Sarov Monastery. For some period of time, he lived in the forest of Sarov Monastery in the cell of the elder Varlaam (†1764), who was the spiritual father of Father Nazarius, the future abbot of Valaam Monastery. In 1778, Egor Ivanovich Popov became a novice at the Sarov Monastery. Little is known about this period in his life. It is clear that before he entered the monastery, he served as junior clerk in the military command of the city of Kadom. Also, he knew the monk Theophan, who in 1771 became a novice in Sanaksarskii Monastery, which is located not far from Sarov. Theophan later became an archimandrite and the superior of the Kyrillo-Novozerskii Monastery. From 1782 to 1791, Theophan served as cell attendant for Metropolitan Gabriel of Novgorod and St Petersburg.

Remembering Father Herman, Archimandrite Theophan wrote, "Father Herman (he is now in America) from the earliest years lived in the forest with Father Varlaam. Once Father Varlaam had to depart and left the youth—he was 12 years old—alone. Those who were gathering mushrooms in the woods lost their way and came across a cell of hermits. When he entered their cell, they were afraid of him, since his presence in the forest seemed so unusual to them."[16]

In his youth, Egor was seriously ill. A tumor formed on his throat that grew quickly and deformed his entire face. The pain was terrible; it was difficult to swallow. The tumor gave off an unbearable odor. Despite this, he did not go to the doctor, but with heartfelt prayer and tears of repentance he fell down before an icon of the Mother of God and began to ask God for healing. He prayed all night, after which he wiped the face of the Most-Holy Mother of God with a wet cloth and then used it to wrap the tumor. Continuing to pray, Egor fell asleep on the floor from exhaustion and saw in a dream that the

Most-Holy Virgin healed him. When he woke up, he was completely healed. The tumor had disappeared without bursting. It left only a small mark on his neck, as if in memory of the miracle.

In 1781, Archbishop Gabriel of Novgorod and St Petersburg decided to assign Hieromonk Nazarius of Sarov Monastery as the superior[17] of Valaam Monastery. There were only four residents of Valaam in the fall of 1781: two married priests, one monk, and Hegumen Ephrem, the superior. The married priests and the monk drowned in the fall of 1781 while crossing Lake Ladoga. Having left for St Petersburg to take care of some affairs of the monastery in January 1782, Hegumen Ephrem was relieved of his responsibilities. Father Ephrem fell ill in St Petersburg and died March 3, 1782. According to a decree of March 7, 1782, Father Nazarius was named superior of Valaam Monastery; at the time, he was on a pilgrimage at Konevsky Monastery. Hieromonk Nazarius and four novices arrived in St Petersburg in January 1782.

The petition for their visas has been preserved:

To the member of the Most-Holy Governing Synod, the Most Reverend Archbishop Gabriel of Novgorod and St Petersburg and the archimandrite of the Holy Trinity Alexander Nevsky Monastery,

From Hicromonk Nazarius of Sarov Monastery of the Vladimir Diocese along with these novices,

A Most Humble Petition:

Due to our zeal we have the desire to visit and venerate the holy places of the St Petersburg Diocese in the Konevsky and Valaam Monasteries that are in Lake Ladoga.

For this sake we most humbly request Your Grace to allow us, the most lowly ones, to travel to the aforementioned monasteries and to live there for as long as we are able, and to deign to issue a passport for travel.

January 1782

Hieromonk Nazarius put his hand to this petition. (signature)

Reserve ensign Basil Apkhipov put his hand to this petition. (signature)

Reserve company clerk Aleksei Vetskoi put his hand to this petition. (signature)

Reserve assistant company clerk Egor Popov put his hand to this petition. (signature)

A member of Kursk lower middle class, Peter Matchin, put his hand to this petition. (signature)

On this document there is the following resolution:

January 12, 1782

To issue the petitioners a passport for pilgrimage at their desire to the Valaam and Konevsky monasteries.[18]

Father Nazarius and the novices arrived at Valaam. The selection of the novices was not by chance; three of the four were army reservists and Basil Apkhipov was even an officer, an ensign. They had already mastered discipline and the careful carrying out of their superior's orders, even in the world. Father Nazarius alone served the services on Valaam for about a year, because there were no other hieromonks there. In November 1782, the novices E. I. Popov and P. Matchin were tonsured into monasticism. The report of their tonsures follows:

To the Most-Holy Governing Synod

A Report

After the decree of Her Majesty from the Most-Holy Governing Synod of October 22 of this year which was sent to me, the assistant company clerk Egor Popov and the member of the Kursk lower middle class Peter Matchin, who are among the brotherhood of the Spaso-Preobrazhenskii Valaam Monastery, were tonsured 1 November and named: Popov—Herman,[19] Matchin—Patermufii, as is stated in the report sent by the superior of that monastery and about which I most respectfully report to the Most-Holy Governing Synod.

The obedient servant of Your Majesty

Gabriel, Archbishop of Novgorod[20]

After a visit to Valaam Monastery in 1785, the academic N. Ia. Ozertskovskii wrote the following vivid description of this monastery and the life of its residents.

In general the location of the monastery is quite beautiful, and, it can said, majestic, but the monastery structures do not correspond to the location in the least. They consist of a wooden fence, inside of which are the church with its bell tower and small monastery huts, which are also wooden. But during my stay there they began to build from stone both a church and monastic cells. . . . The current hermits lead a labor-loving life. The slightest disagreement is not seen in their community, which consists of at least twenty people. They possess nothing as individuals; instead they own everything together. But most commendable of all is their sobriety. . . . There is no other settlement on the entire island of Valaam, except for the monastery. In various places only huts exist, deliberately situated for the greater solitude of the Valaam hermits, some of whom withdraw from their brothers to the huts and live there for several weeks or months at a time. The places chosen for these retreats are only the most beautiful ones where the vista encompasses a pleasant view of trees, plants, stone cliffs, and valleys, and where the soul is fed by the meditations to which silence and solitude give birth.

With an adequate supply of all that is necessary for life and while living in complete silence and tranquility, these hermits lead a blessed life and have compelling reason to conduct themselves according to their calling. In fairness, it is impossible not to give them credit for this, since they are well behaved and conduct the cycle of services every day. They all eat lunch and dinner together; moreover, they typically observe absolute silence, for the keeping of which one of the brotherhood stands and reads loudly and clearly from some religious book while the brothers eat. Their diet typically consists of cabbage soup, fish soup, and meal. They do not dish these liquids into bowls, but instead scoop them up with wooden spoons from large wooden bowls; they do not hold napkins for cleaning up. . . . At meals, the youngest waits upon them. At the end of the meal, they all read a prayer out loud together and depart for their cells. There they practice various handiwork, such as turning maple spoons, carving cypress crosses, and the like, while in the summer they work in vegetable gardens, till the soil, harvest wheat, and cut hay. The superior, Nazarius, participates in all these jobs with the others.[21]

Under the leadership of Father Nazarius, Valaam Monastery was transformed. The old wooden structures were replaced with stone ones. The Dormition Church was built of stone in 1785; in 1793, St Nicholas Church; and in 1794, the Transfiguration Church along with its bell tower and the skete with the Church of All Saints. The brotherhood of the Novgorod Dukhovnii monastery was transferred to Valaam in 1786; their former monastery became a convent. In that same year, Valaam Monastery was added to the list of established monasteries of the third class with hegumen superiors, and its superior, Father Nazarius, was raised to the rank of hegumen.

Father Varlaam, a contemporary of Father Herman's who later became superior of Valaam, recalled this about the life of the saint at Valaam: "Father Herman undertook various obediences here and, by the way, as 'one ready for any good deed,' was sent to the town of Serdobol'[22] to supervise the granite quarrying there. The brothers loved

Father Herman and anxiously awaited his return from Serdobol' to the community."[23]

Despite the fact that Valaam was a very strict monastery, the soul of Father Herman sought solitude, and, after experience in various obediences, Father Nazarius released him to live in a hermitage.

The book *Valaam Monastery and Its Ascetics*,[24] published in 1899, describes the hermits:

As far as those Valaam monks are concerned—those who have received a blessing from the monastery leadership to seek their salvation in hermitages due to the trustworthy testimony of their lives—these strict ascetics, instead of attending daily divine services, continually practice prayer in their cells, especially the prayer of the mind. They keep a monastic prayer rule as prescribed by ancient statutes. For the maintenance of their life and strength, they are content with the most meager food, which they prepare themselves.

The hermits, like the skete-dwellers, come to the monastery on great feast days regardless of the kind of weather. There they are lovingly received by the brothers, participate with them in the common services, and share in a meal.

The quantity and state of the prayer of the hermits, as ones already experienced in the spiritual life, depends entirely on the degree of their strength and the internal movements of their soul. These elements, however, are dependably checked by the prudent sense and conscience of the superior or spiritual father of those being guided, since this is a priest's responsibility, and is confirmed by the hermits' way of life. Therefore the hermits' service to God is concealed, like their lives. But they are hidden, according to scripture, "with Christ in God" (Col 3:3).[25]

The hermitage, which Father Herman chose for himself, was located in a deep forest, a little more than a mile from the monastery. That place is called "Herman's field"[26] to this day. Father Herman lived alone in the hermitage for a period of time, and subsequently he lived with the young novice Kuz'ma Alekseevich Telepnev, just as he had lived in his youth at Sarov Monastery in the cell of elder Varlaam. In 1793, at the time of his departure from Valaam, Father Herman was forty-two years old, and the novice K. A. Telepnev was twenty years old. On holidays, Father Herman would walk from the hermitage to the monastery. Tears would pour from his eyes during small vespers while standing on the kliros and singing along with the brothers the refrains of the canon: "O sweetest Jesus, save us sinners" and "O most holy Mother of God save us."

Judging by their letters, Father Herman personally knew Metropolitan Gabriel of Novgorod, St Petersburg, and Olonets when he was a ruling hierarch of the Russian Orthodox Church. By 1793, Father Herman had been invited to be ordained as a priest-monk and even to be made archimandrite and head of the Russian Orthodox mission in Peking. It was again suggested that he become a priest-monk in 1808, but "he did not want to be an archimandrite, understanding well that with every elevation he would be more and more bound and further and further from his favorite occupation: to praise God as a hermit!"[27]

Father Herman spent ten years in Valaam Monastery in the unceasing ascetic struggles of fasting and prayer, but it would become more pleasing to God that he serve at the other end of the earth—in Alaska—among a people who had not yet come to know the true faith.

CHAPTER 2

Missionary Service in Alaska

ORGANIZATION OF THE ORTHODOX MISSION IN AMERICA

Alaska was discovered in 1741 by the Russian sailors Vitus Jonassen Bering[28] and A. I. Chirikovii. The economic development of this territory began in 1745 in the Aleutian chain. Beginning in the 1780s, several trading and trapping companies won monopolies from the government for the exploitation of Alaska. One of them was headed by the merchants Ivan Larionovich Golikov and Grigorii Ivanovich Shelikhov.[29] In 1784, Shelikhov set out for Alaska, where he stayed until 1786. He founded a permanent settlement on Kodiak Island, subjugating the local population to himself. Shelikhov transferred to Siberia fifteen residents of Kodiak and the regions near it. Two of them, Alakhan and Kiiak, were lodged in Golikov's house in Kursk. They were baptized in 1789.

The petition of Alakhan and Kiiak "to join the Ortho-dox Greek-Russian Church" notes that "we, the under-signed, were born in the very distant, recently discovered American territory, one of us on an island and the other on the mainland. We lived like the wild peoples who reside there, not knowing any faith or law and not hav-ing the least understanding of any Divinity; we grew up in complete ignorance of the true God." In baptism, Alakhan was named Peter and Kiiak, Paul. Both Ameri-cans subsequently continued to live in Kursk and to serve Golikov.[30]

In 1789, Metropolitan Gabriel decided to send two monks to serve in America. The two chosen for this purpose were the monk Iakov, for whom there are no records of the monastery in which he lived, and Hieromonk Joachim from Sarov Monastery. "But this one [Joachim], who loved Sarov monastery and the spiritual poverty of simple monasticism, began to decline such an appointment, and even acted as a 'fool-for-Christ' for several years in order to avoid such an honor."[31]

Having received this news from abbot Pakhomii of Sarov monastery, Metropolitan Gabriel wrote,

> Having read your letter, I was shocked. Father Joachim, who is worthy of Christian love, behaves this way, as you write, in order to save himself. But he who does not want to aid in the salvation of others, is not saving himself.

Humility, which he always preserves in his soul, will rise up, when, having been called to the salvation of many, he will be like a slave and servant.

I ask you to admonish him in the name of Jesus Christ, who took the sins of the entire world, that he follow in His footsteps. He came into the world to a throng of corrupt people, so that He could save them. Surely he does not think this example is not worthy of imitation? Does he say that we have no strength and are weak? The Apostle Paul said this, but then he confessed: "yet not I, but the grace of God which was with me" (1 Cor 15:10).

Christ is calling him; grace awaits him, so that he can work with it. Let him consider, what a great transgression this is—to make your ears deaf to the call of Jesus Christ.[32]

At this time, the idea to send monks to serve in America did not come to fruition.

In 1793, Golikov and Shelikov personally appealed to the Most-Holy Synod with a petition in which they asked to send "a good priest with the necessary assistants" to America. The ober-procurator of the synod made a report to Catherine II, who ordered that not one priest but a whole Orthodox mission be sent to America.

Metropolitan Gabriel of Novgorod, St Petersburg, and Olonets was entrusted with creating the mission. Metropolitan Gabriel, knowing the ascetic life of the Valaam elders, their unshakable devotion to Orthodoxy, and readiness to undertake any labor in the name of God,

charged Hegumen Nazarius to select a few monks to fulfill this very important obedience. Monk Herman immediately volunteered to go to America. Hegumen Nazarius
assigned a total of six monks and four novices to the mission. Archimandrite Joseph headed the mission. Subordinate to him were Hieromonks[33] Juvenaly, Macarius,
and Athanasius; Hierodeacon Nectarios and monk Herman; and the four novices Kuz'ma Alekseevich Telepnev,
Michael Fedorovich Govorukhin, Nikita Semenov, and
Dmitry Avdeev. Only a little is known about their lives
before they arrived in America.

Archimandrite Joseph (in the world Ivan Il'ich
Bolotov), the son of a village priest, was born in the village of Strazhkovo in the Tver province on January 22,
1761 (according to other sources, he was born in 1757).
He studied in the Tver Seminary until theology classes
began, when he transferred to the Yaroslav Seminary and
finished the full course. He taught for four years in the
Uglich Theological School. In 1786 or 1787, he accepted
monasticism with the name Joseph in the Tolga Monastery in Yaroslav, from which he moved to the Iugskaya
Dorofeevskaya Hermitage. In 1792, at his request, he was
transferred to Valaam.

Hieromonk Juvenaly (in the world Iakov Fedorovich Govorukhin) was born in 1761 in Yekaterinburg. He
worked in the Nerchinsk mining factories as an assistant
engineer. In 1791, he was accepted into the Valaam Monastery and was tonsured in 1793.

Hieromonk Macarius (in the world Matvei Aleksandrov) was born to serfs in 1750 in the village of Chayanki, Orlov province. In 1770, he became a monk in the Bogoroditskaya Ploshchahskaya Hermitage of the Orlov Diocese and in 1793 was transferred to the Konev Monastery of the St Petersburg Diocese.

Hieromonk Athanasius (in the world Anton Semenovich Michaelov) was born in 1758 to serfs. In 1785, he became a novice at Valaam. In 1788, he was tonsured a monk, and in 1793 he was ordained a hierodeacon.

Hierodeacon Nectarios (in the world Feodor Dimitrievich Panov) was born in 1762 to merchants from the city of Kostroma. From 1787 to 1791, he was a novice in the Sarov Monastery and transferred to Valaam in 1791. In 1792, he was tonsured a monk and elevated to the deaconate.

Novice Michael Feodorovich Govorukhin was the brother of Hieromonk Juvenaly. He worked in the Nerchinsk mining factories. He became a novice in the Konevsky Monastery, from which he was transferred to Valaam in 1793.

Novice Kuz'ma Alekseevich Telepnev was born in 1773 in the city of Serpukhov. It is possible that at the age of sixteen he became a novice at Holy Trinity–St Sergius Hermitage outside of St Petersburg and from there was transferred to Valaam Monastery. It is known that the abbot of Valaam Monastery, Father Nazarius, visited Holy Trinity–St Sergius Hermitage sometime in the 1780s or 1790s and was extremely dissatisfied with the internal order of this monastery. The two other novices, Dmitry Avdeev and Nikita Semenov, were also from Valaam.

A truly great deed befell the lot of these men chosen by divine providence. Ioann E. Veniaminov (Bishop Innocent from 1840, and from 1868 Metropolitan of Moscow and Kolomensk, now glorified among the saints as the Hierarch Innocent of Moscow) wrote,

> It is indeed a holy endeavor, one equal to that of the apostles, to leave your homeland and go to places that are remote, wild, and devoid of many of the comforts of life in order to convert to the path of Truth people who are still wandering in the darkness of ignorance and to illumine with the light of the Gospel those who still have not seen this saving light. Blessed is he whom the Lord chooses and places in such service!
>
> But especially blessed is he who with all fervor, sincerity, and love struggles to convert and to enlighten, enduring the labors and sorrows met in the course of his service, for great is his reward in the heavens.[34]

The mission departed from St Petersburg in December 1793, its route passing through Moscow to Irkutsk. The fathers arrived in Irkutsk on March 16, 1794, and stayed there until May 2.

In Irkutsk, the monks met Shelikhov. He gave Archimandrite Joseph the plan of the church that was to be built on Kodiak, along with church supplies, clothing, and provisions for several months. The novice Michael Govorukhin was tonsured a monk in Irkutsk on April 20 and given the name Stephen. On April 30, he was ordained as a hierodeacon.

Shelikhov wrote a letter to Alexander Andreevich Baranov, the chief manager of his settlement in America, concerning the construction of the church: "Select a place for the church so that, as far as possible, half of it is either inside the settlement or facing the homes of the locals, so that it will be possible to enter the church from them without going into the other half, which should remain outside the settlement and be enclosed by a strong and tall bulwark; this half should be large enough to hold cells for the priest-archimandrite and other monastics, along with the necessary amenities, a garden and a school for young Americans."[35]

Shelikhov was more open in a secret instruction to Baranov. He ordered a monastery and church for the mission to be built in such a way "that the monks don't see what the laity are doing; and the laity don't see what the monks are doing."[36]

Shelikhov planned to use the monks for secular work. In part, he hoped that Father Juvenaly and Father Stephen, because they "knew the mathematical sciences," would help in the construction of a new fortress and in the building of a forge. He wrote, "For a start it would be enough if in the near future you had found iron and copper ores, since they are necessary for the newly established settlement and shipbuilding. Get instructions from Father Juvenaly and Father Stephen about how to smelt them, what kind of smelting furnaces to build, and how to set up everything else, since they are skilled in mining and industrial science."[37]

Shelikhov also intended to transfer supervision of the school that was already being run on Kodiak to the mission. He wrote, "Those young boys you have on Kodiak who are studying reading and writing, entrust to the study of reading, writing, and mathematics under the direction of the archimandrite, since among the brothers subordinate to him there are several who have the ability to be teachers and readily expressed their desire to do so here, particularly Father Macarius."[38]

The monks left Irkutsk on May 2. Their path lay along the River Lena to Yakutsk and from there on horseback to Okhotsk, where they arrived June 13. They remained in Okhotsk for a month. Three days before their departure for America, the monks sent a final letter from Russia to Metropolitan Gabriel:

Most Eminent Master!
   Most Merciful Archpastor and father!
   It would be audacious to be so bold as to disturb Your Eminence with news of our arrival, such little people as we are, knowing how occupied you are with important affairs, if we did not know your fatherly kindness to us and your special concern, which is accompanied by an equable condescension.

Rejoicing in this, we informed you in a letter to Your Eminence at the start of spring of our arrival in Irkutsk and our stay there. Now we are bold to inform you that aided by your hierarchical prayers, having overcome the difficulty of an uncomfortable horseback ride both from Irkutsk to Yakutsk as well as from there to Okhotsk, we arrived in Okhotsk on July 12. We are all well and to our pleasure heard new news from America—a company ship arrived from Chugatskaia Bay on the mainland on which there were nine Americans. They assure us that not only on the islands, but also on the mainland, no danger should be expected from those distant residents, and that even at Chugatskaia Bay they began to build a company ship.

Grigorii Ivanovich Shelikhov traveled with us to Okhotsk. He obtained for us all that is required not only for the church, but also for our upkeep. As a result, we will have no great needs for three years, as long as, God forbid, some unforeseen disaster does not require us to send ships from Okhotsk to America.

It can be hoped that in the next few days we will set sail and if God will help, we will reach America. Then we will not miss the first opportunity to inform Your Eminence in detail about the conditions there.

In conclusion, most humbly asking your archpastoral prayers and blessings, and the continuation of your fatherly kindness to us and with the utmost respect and deepest devotion, we have the honor and joy to always remain,

of Your Eminence,

Most Merciful Archpastor and father!

the most humble, devoted servants: Archimandrite Joseph, Hieromonk Juvenaly, Hieromonk Macarius, Hieromonk Athanasius, Hierodeacon Nectarios, Hierodeacon Stephen, monk Herman.

Okhotsk.

August 10, 1794[39]

The monks departed for America on August 13 on the vessel *The Three Saints*.[40] The ship held 126 people in all: ten members of the mission, five Aleuts, forty-five people from settler families, a navigator, an assistant to Baranov, two stewards, and sixty-two *promyshlenniki*.[41]

This was the first time the members of the mission encountered those people with whom they were to live for many years in Alaska. "The overwhelming majority of these men were Russian northerners or Siberian descendants of the Pomory.[42] They were predominantly free peasants, or Siberian townsmen, with their own notions of social order, community, leadership, labor relations, religious community structure, and marriage."

The majority of the *promyshlenniki* were broke speculators, runaway peasants, released convicts, and soldiers. Shelikhov's company tried to sign up people who were already burdened by debts. They were paid in such a way that even before their arrival in America, they had a sizable debt to the company and were entirely dependent on it. The recruiting of *promyshlenniki* for service in America was accompanied by great revelry in Okhotsk. "When

hired in the service of the company the workers ... were to
be found in a perversion of the human figure, manifested
by both daily drunkenness and disorderliness, which the
police were powerless to stop."[43]

At the start of September, the ship made a stop at
Unalaska Island, where the missionary labors of the
monks in America began. Archimandrite Joseph's letter
of May 19, 1795, to Hegumen Nazarius at Valaam provides a picture of what met them in Alaska:

> Having traveled by sea along the Aleutian chain only two days,
> we stopped in at Unalaska Island and baptized more than a
> hundred people there: they have long been ready to receive
> baptism, since they continually live with Russian *promyshlen-*
> *niki*. This past winter on Kodiak we baptized more than 6,000
> people. They accepted baptism with such zeal that they shred-
> ded and burned their shamanistic attire.
>
> Although you scared us about nudity; they do, thank God,
> have a concept of modesty. Though not elegant, all the same
> they dress no less immodestly and neatly than Russians: the
> poor wear dresses made from bird skins, but down to the feet
> and the same for each sex, like a sticharion.[44] There is one
> opening—only for the head to go through. When they dress
> up they wear beaver-skin dresses. Their food is fish and vari-
> ous roots.[45]

The Aleuts, dissatisfied with the short visit of the
mission, asked Archimandrite Joseph to leave one of the

hieromonks on Unalaska. He promised them that one of the monks would visit them soon.

On September 24, 1794, *The Three Saints* arrived in the settlement at Pavlovskaia Harbor on Kodiak Island. From this date, the spread of Orthodoxy among the native population of Alaska began.

FIRST YEAR ON KODIAK ISLAND

The native population of Kodiak and the neighboring islands were Kodiak Eskimos. Russians called them *Americans*, and later came to call them *Aleuts*, by extension from the residents of the Aleutian Islands, whom they had met before the residents of Kodiak Island. The Kodiak Aleutians were in an oppressed condition; in essence, they were serfs of Shelikhov's company. The difference between them and peasant serfs in Russia was that they could not be sold and they were not farmers, but hunters of marine animals. Later, the Kodiak Aleuts were officially included in the class of free peasants.

Along with *The Three Saints*, the vessel *Saint Catherine* put in on Kodiak. A total of 193 people were on these ships. Alexander Andreevich Baranov did not have resources to house and feed such a large quantity of people. The winter of 1794–1795 was very difficult. During their first winter in America, the villager Philip Tiapkin helped the missionaries with particular zeal.[46]

Soon after arriving on Kodiak, the novice Kuz'ma Alekseev was tonsured a monk and given the name

Joseph. The foundation of the church was laid on November 21, 1794. Archimandrite Joseph gave the monks obediences according to their abilities: Father Macarius was assigned to missionary work among the Kodiak Aleuts. He traveled to numerous settlements over the course of two months, baptized close to 6,000 people, and married several hundred couples. Osip A. Prianishnikov accompanied him as a translator.

Osip Andreevich Prianishnikov, a merchant from Tobolsk, was assigned to be the translator for the mission after its arrival. He had recently returned from a hunting expedition of 500 *baidarkas*[47] which had been headed by Egor Purtovii and Demid Kulikalovii to Yaktusk Bay, during which he led negotiations with Yakut chief Kuan. By the arrival of Baranov in 1791, Prianishnikov already knew Kodiak, Aleut, and Chugach Yupik. From that time on, he accompanied the manager[48] on his expeditions and participated in June 1792 in repelling the night raid of the Yakutat Tlingits on Baranov's party. The next year he accompanied E. Purtov's party to Mount St Elias. Even before the arrival of the archimandrite with the fathers, "knowing the order of divine services, he led morning services, hours, and evening services." Henceforth, being attached to the mission, he not only translated, but also fulfilled the duties of a reader.[49]

With the arrival of the mission, "with great zeal he firmly established himself in the preaching of the Gospel." Prianishnikov's service as a translator had lasting success, because "he is loved and respected by all the residents of Kodiak for his respectable life and gentle treatment of them."[50]

Father Nectarios directed the school, in which fifteen students studied. Among them were children of Kodiak Aleuts, Creoles, and hostages, which even included Tlingits.[51] Father Juvenaly and Father Stephen undertook the construction of the church, in addition to conducting services in Pavlovskaia Harbor.[52] Father Herman and Father Joseph were assigned to the bakery, and Father Athanasius, as the least capable, was assigned to take care of the vegetable garden and to study divine services.

In the spring of 1795, Archimandrite Joseph devoted special attention to the cultivation of the gardens. He wrote, "I would like to start at least a little potato, cabbage, and some other garden vegetables; the main problem with this is that we do not have proper tools. I have asked [Baranov] to at least make some spades or hoes, but I do not know if anything will come of it. For now, we are managing to work the soil with sharpened wooden chocks."[53]

Archimandrite Joseph informed Father Ieronim, rector of the Yaroslav Seminary, about his fellow missionaries:

> My brotherhood is most kind. Many of them you know yourself, my brother: the hermit Herman . . . there is someone with whom to spend time; the humble hermit Athanasius is already a hieromonk. The Siberian who was at Valaam, Iakov Fedorov, now Hieromonk Juvenaly, is a good man. Perhaps you remember Hierodeacon Macarius from Konevsky, who

was at Valaam for the feast of St Peter? He is a hieromonk, a humble man. Kuz'ma Alekseev, who lived with Herman in the hermitage, is now Joseph, a smart man. . . . Hierodeacon Stephen, you can't wish for a better man than him. We even have two novices, young men, who read and sing well. . . . We run a school here, and there are already several boys, offspring of affairs between Russian *promyshlenniki* and American women, who know how to read and come to the choir to sing.[54]

The first ten months of the monks' life in America are described in detail in several letters: Archimandrite Joseph's to Metropolitan Gabriel of May 19, 1795; Archimandrite Joseph's to Shelikhov of May 18, 1795; and Father Herman's to Hegumen Nazarius. Selections from the first two letters follow; the third is included in its entirety.

Report of Archimandrite Joseph
    To the Archbishop concerning conditions
    in the Russian settlement on Kodiak Island.[55]
    Your Grace, Vladyka,[56]
    Most honorable archbishop and father.

We entered the ocean from Okhotsk August 13, 1794. Although we encountered several storms, with the aid of your holy prayers we still successfully arrived in north-west America, to Kodiak Island, on September 24.

Following your Grace's instructions for us, we tried, through translators, to give the Americans some elementary understanding of God and His Holy faith. However, many problems exist which hinder the Americans from accepting Holy Baptism. Due to our demand that they abandon polygamy, they are deprived of many benefits. But, admitting the holiness of the Christian faith, they are agreeable to give their extra wives to others.

I cannot baptize them until they have been introduced to the Gospel laws and they understand their meaning. Yet due to their ardent pleas, I do not wait until they are ready for baptism. I have also noticed, that those who were baptized before do not abandon their old habits, but continue to respect shamans and use pagan rituals. They rightfully say of themselves that they cannot be baptized due to their behavior. They also condemn the bad behavior of those who have been recently baptized. . . .

Therefore, I baptize everyone who comes to the settlement of Pavlovskaia Harbor and expresses a desire to be baptized. I only try to confirm how much they understand. I explain the rules of Christian life to them. Due to the great distance from Pavlovskaia Harbor [to the Aleut settlements], 300 or more versts,[57] most Americans from youths to the elderly were baptized by the two Hieromonks Markarii and Juvenaly, who were sent by me to travel around the island [Kodiak] to baptize the Americans. They prepared a report, which was sent to His Grace Veniamin, Bishop of Irkutsk and Nerchensk.

If we are not able to speak the local languages, then our efforts to spread the Orthodox faith will run into great problems, but, unfortunately, even a translator is not able to properly express even in his own words the reason for our teaching to the Americans in their own language. We have not had the opportunity to study their language. Each tribe speaks in its own dialect: Kodiak, Alaskan, Kenai, Chugash, Koliuzh, and other tribes which live along the shore, each speak in different languages and not one of them resembles the other.

We have no opportunity to speak more openly about the Christian life even with the recently baptized residents of Kodiak, because only a few of them live in the village of Pavlovskaia Harbor. Moreover, besides the portion of residents who have come here from the mainland, those who are assigned to work for the company or are temporary guests [in Pavlovskaia Harbor], the other Americans live in settlements that are far from the island. Weather conditions do not allow us to visit them often, in addition to which there are no roads to these settlements. Everywhere along the coastline you run into inaccessible mountains, volcanoes, and harbors with steep shores.

The number of newly baptized on Kodiak is more than 6,000 people; this is almost everyone [Kodiaks], beside those about which there is some doubt:

1. *Zhupani*, that is, men who were raised from childhood as women and fulfill all obligations of women, so that Americans keep them as wives. They wish to be baptized, but do not abandon their foul vice.

2. Polygamy is practiced in all local settlements. When a man takes himself a tart, he keeps her as long as he wants. If he, or the girl, does not want to live together anymore,

they separate and freely take someone else. These sort of people come to us to be baptized, but when they hear that we do not allow polygamy and easy divorces, then even those who already have children renounce their children and their former wives. They are willing to have just one wife and to not divorce her until death, if they are allowed to pick a new wife and then come to be baptized and married with this new wife. They abandon their old wives and children with regret.

3.   There are Americans who have intimate relations with their relatives: cousins, nieces, and even a few with their own daughters, from whom they have begotten children that they raise together. Such people also come and ask for baptism, but under the condition that I allow them to marry the woman with whom they are living, even if they are close blood relatives.

4.   Among the Russian *promyshlenniki* there are those who have lived in America for fifteen years or more. They have left a wife behind in Russia and keep a concubine here, with whom they have begotten children. They ask to baptize these women and to be allowed to marry them. They say that they have lost hope to return to Russia. They openly admit that [they] came to such a distant land because they had argued with their wives.

Unfortunately, I do not have the right, without your Grace's permission, to baptize or marry these Americans. Therefore I ask you to send me specific instructions about how to behave in these circumstances.[58]

In his letter to Shelikhov, Archimandrite Joseph wrote,

The only satisfaction to be had is that Americans converge from every quarter to be baptized. And the Russians not only do not try to encourage them in this, but use every means to dissuade them. The reason for this is that their depraved life began to be exposed by the good behavior of the Americans. I could barely convince a few of the *promyshlenniki* to marry, and others will not even listen. But they all keep women openly. Moreover, they keep not just one, which serves as a great offense to the Americans. . . .

From the time of our arrival, all that they regale us with is sun-dried, three-year-old salmon. . . . There are no provisions even for the others who have moved here. Once I sent one of my monks to the barracks of the new settlers; he saw that they were all overcrowded. They do not have enough supplies either, though they spend entire nights straight through in drinking bouts and binges, singing and dancing. On the first Wednesday of Great Lent they refused to go to confession until they had finished a binge.

I have yet to find out if my arrival or your sharp reproofs, written to Mr Baranov, enraged him or not. . . . There is nothing good to note in the living conditions. . . . The constantly half-naked, barefoot cooks make a mess all day, feed people, and at night chop wood. We even have to carry our own [firewood] from the woods on our shoulders. All the more humorous is the fact that even the manager does not have wood chopped for the whole year. When they need to heat the teapot at his house, they either run around the building to break off some coal or to the barn to steal a board. And sometimes they take charcoal from the forge, until the teapot is ready. I have yet to see him go out to look over something being done; day and night he sits and occupies himself with various chicanery. . . .

There are only five children studying. And almost all the former students live in the quarters without supervision and fool around, so that they do not differ from the others at all. . . .

I baptize Americans, not making any impediments to the company in any way, since serfs remain serfs, hostages remain hostages, and every *promyshlennik* keeps his job. And the fact that he is baptized, it would seem, does no harm, but it always creates some difficulty for me.

While baptizing in the villages, it has happened that the very same Aleuts and the women they keep have been baptized and married, but then incidents have sometimes occurred, so that [Russians] took away several women who had been married by me to be their concubines. . . .

The letter continues about Baranov:

He [Baranov] said, "I have an order from Shelikhov to support the religious mission with extreme austerity, to accustom them to the local diet, to use them for all sorts of work and so on."

And so, without your instructions, necessity forces us to learn to get used to the local diet and to keep no hope of using many provisions. We frequent the table open to all: in the tideland we gather mussels and sea snails. Without these, we would be left with bread alone, and that will not last for long. . . .

The winter was cold; the rooms are not caulked; and the little windows are bad. We struggled through the entire winter this way. It is true that since my arrival he [Baranov] has paid me the respect of setting aside good quarters—for me only and assigning the brotherhood to the barracks, where visitors stay with their concubines. But I could not think to let the brotherhood live with them. So we all moved to different rooms, since besides the fact that the barracks are full of concubines, there are gatherings, frequent carousing, and dancing all night. There is so much that they don't even stop on Sundays and feast days.

And again he writes about Baranov:

Although he assigned 1,500 [rubles] in the books for the church as well as for the retinue, it would have been more tolerable for me if he would have taken that much from me; I would have managed things better here. . . .

The *promyshlenniki*, by permission of the manager, take children begotten by Russians from their mothers, and, furthermore, the children are so young that some are just a year and others are two-year-olds—and they are going to send them to Russia. I don't like this very much. . . .

I have heard from several people that Baranov often tells his ruffians: "How I would like to send the archimandrite to the other world, along with Juvenaly; then we would squash the others like flies." Although I should not believe all idle talk, I cannot but doubt that from someone so inhuman it could happen. He has surely already sent people to the other world, so he would not hesitate to send me. This past Pascha they marched one serf through a gauntlet of pummeling whalebones, killing him.[59]

Upon his arrival in Alaska, Father Herman wrote Hegumen Nazarius at Valaam,

My most-reverend and most-worthy Father Superior, Father Nazarius, along with all our brothers in Christ: Rejoice in the Lord!

Your fatherly benefactions to me, a wretch, will not be erased from my heart neither by terrifying, impassable, Siberian places, nor by dark forests; they will not be washed away by the rapids of great rivers; these feelings will not be extinguished even by the dread ocean.

In my mind I see my beloved Valaam; I always look at it across the great ocean. And with my own voice, it is not possible, due to the great distance, to proclaim, as is my duty, my gratitude. But by means of this small piece of paper, I am trying, as much as possible, to express that to you, my kind father. Notwithstanding this, I beg to report something about myself.

1. Through the Grace of the Most-High God, by your holy prayers, we reached American territory safely, all ten of us. The lack of time does not allow me to describe in detail so great a journey. We spent almost the entire year on the road. We met

no adventures worthy of recollection, except for a few due to the novelty of the places or the variety of means of travel. Except perhaps for the sake of simple conversation, you can tell those who love news, that bears attacked us while riding horseback along the Okhotsk road and that we came across various sea creatures while on the ocean: whales, killer whales, dolphins, Stellar sea lions, and others—we saw many of all these. There were no strong gales, except for one.

2. We live on Kodiak Island, but in a temporary settlement. Our intention is to move to the mainland, but we do not know where we would like to be. The Americans come for baptism very willingly. A few less than 7,000 have been baptized. During the voyage along the Aleutian Islands, we were driven unwillingly into a harbor on Unalaska by opposing winds; the Aleuts surprised us with their gentleness and desire for baptism.

3. Father Macarius, along with this letter, is currently being sent to preach and baptize in the Aleutian, Lisyevskii, and Andreevskii Islands. And then, in the near future, Father Juvenaly will head to the mainland, beginning at Kenai Bay, to visit the Chugach, the Alegmiut, the remote Kolosh [Tlingit], and many other tribes, even the Chilkhat. Oh! The spirit of this event has so captivated me, that despite the extreme lack of time, I will snatch a brief moment to add some details to the continuation of this story.

We live between a bucket and bad weather, between joy and tedium, between plenty and privation, satisfaction and hunger, warmth and cold. With all my sorrows, I find nothing so cheers me as when I hear discussions among the brothers about preaching and about dividing various regions among themselves for that purpose, particularly a debate between Hieromonks Macarius and Juvenaly. For they had set out around Kodiak in the smallest sort of hide-covered boats, in spite of the dangers of the sea, and Father Archimandrite [Joseph] stayed with us, as if with little children in the Harbor [in the settlement of Pavlovskaia Harbor].

The monks developed their ideas further once while walking in our harbor, when I, a sinner, happened to be with them. We walked up to a small hill on the southern side, to look at the ocean, and, incidentally, we began to discuss where each of us should go to preach, since the time was approaching for the departure of the ships on which we were to travel. And at that time an argument arose between them, which was a consolation and a joy for a wretch like me.

Kukovskii's maps indicate that Russian people live in the north along one river. We had heard various rumors about them, which we then recalled, among other conversation, since we wished to see them somehow.

Father Macarius spoke first:

"It is my intention, if God allows, when I will be in the Aleutian Islands, that out of propriety I should also go to Alaska [the Alaskan peninsula], for the Alaskans have already invited me there, and since those Russians are closer to that area, then I will look for a way to find out about them with certainty."

Then Father Juvenaly, having heard about Alaska and from jealousy being unable to let that be spoken any more, with an urgent spirit said:

"Alaska, in its entirety, belongs to my part, so I humbly ask you to not offend me by saying otherwise. Since a ship is now departing for Iakutat, then I must begin preaching in the south, and, moving along the ocean to the north and covering Kenai Bay, I will surely enter Alaska through that very harbor."

Hearing this, Father Macarius was overcome with despondency and, assuming a grieved look, said touchingly:

"No, father, do not crowd me, for as you well know the Aleutian Island chain joins with Alaska, so that it surely belongs to my part along with the entire shore north of there. The southern part of America, if you please, will be enough for you for your entire life."

And I, the least of men, listening to such a debate, became delirious with joy. Oh! It is a pity, father, that due to a lack of time I cannot tell you more. I cannot tell you in detail about the morals, customs, and conduct of these regions and about the brotherhood itself.

We tonsured Kuz'ma Alekseevich, changing his name to Joseph. We are in the bakery together. Forgive me, kind father; forgive me, but there is no more time to write. Asking your holy, fatherly prayers and blessings, I remain,

Wretched Herman

I sincerely bow down to all the kind and most-dear Valaam brotherhood and ask their holy prayers.

19th day of May, 1795. Kad'iak[60, 61]

Three days after he wrote this first letter to Hegumen Nazarius, Father Herman wrote another letter:

My most-reverend and most-worthy, merciful superior, Father Nazarius, with all the kind brotherhood in the Lord, I wish for you to rejoice.

I wrote you one general letter, which was to be given to father archimandrite for delivery to you through the partners and which he was certain to read. Due to that, I could not write in it the fact that you could find out about our situation through His Grace [Metropolitan Gabriel], to whom I wrote confidentially about many things; please be so kind as to deal with them. Among others, I mentioned those Russians, but I did not say how they got here.

These are the rumors in the air here: that they are Novgorodians and that during the time of Tsar Ivan Vasil'evich[62] they went to Siberia and, having traveled down the Lena River, they arrived at the Kolyma River. There they built seven ships, called *kocha*,[63] and from the Kolyma crossed over to the Anadyr' River. One ship wrecked there, from which people escaped to the shore, began to live there, and built a church, of which the floor is still whole to this day; they built the current town of Anadyrsk. The other ships went to sea; five stopped at Izhig and Iakum before landing at Tainska, but the sixth disappeared without a trace. What I think is that undoubtedly that ship brought them to America and that they live here, where we currently hear of them. And while composing this little letter of mine, when I had very quietly written up to this point in my small kitchen, I went to the room in which the brotherhood lives, and in which services are conducted in lieu of a church, and through which people continually pass, and there I heard from those who had come from the mainland from the Lebedevskii company, that those Russians are not far from them. And although they have not yet met, it is often said that they have received from others large knives bearing an inscription that certainly belongs to those Russians. They live, it is said, on a large river and the fish in it are Siberian river fish, which we do not have on Kodiak. They even have Russian fish, pike and burbot. If only, dear father, there were some kind of aid from the Tsar, then a great amount of good could be accomplished, for it is very awkward to mix the local people with the merchants, because they are only concerned about wealth and greatly offend the poor Americans, about which I wrote more extensively to His Grace.

I beg you, Father Superior: please, if you have any sympathy to my report, help the poor native people. I particularly asked His Eminence that he send us a bishop or Father Joachim from Sarov or Father Theophan[64] the bishop's former cell attendant, because, it seems to me, that they are not at all concerned about material things, and we desperately need this, so as to not be stingy. But, on the other hand, Father Joachim is elderly and not used to troubles; it seems to me it would be burdensome for him. So, I would very, very much wish for Father Theophan and I think that he would not be bored; due to his nature it could even be very lively, for we always have news and conversation.

Almost as exceptional hieromonks, Father Macarius and Father Juvenaly are always burning with zeal and rushing in all directions. Father Athanasius stays home for us so that we are not without a hieromonk. He both serves the services and baptizes those who come to be baptized. And if only there were no insults to the Americans from the company, then everything would be quite cheery.

Although bread is scarce here, it is possible that wheat would grow if some effort was put forth—we could search for suitable locations.

Even so, the current manager of the company, Baranov, is a wealthy man, in addition to being proud, thoroughly elegant, and not one to make even a small amount of effort about such concerns. You won't believe what kind of foppishness we have here; surely the like of it is not to be found in Russian towns. Our harbor is exactly like some small European town. We recently cast a small five-pood[65] bell and they ring it for every service; in the morning and evenings they beat a drum and play a flute for reveille.

The services are held in our quarters; the beginnings of a small wooden church are done, but it is not finished yet. On holidays the services are attended by *promyshlenniki*, the settlers who came with us, along with the manager, stewards, and navigators, and even officers.

We have turnips, potatoes, and all the garden vegetables growing, but we did not attempt to plant cucumbers or even wheat. One *promyshlennik* planted a pound of barley one summer and harvested one and a half poods;[66] but another planted it and got nothing. Due to the sea fog nothing sprouted.

Forgive me, dear father, forgive me! I grieve sorely and regret that I cannot tell you more; the ship is already about to raise its sail. I bow down before all the kind and most generous Valaam brotherhood. Father Joseph, the former Kuz'ma Alekseevich, lives with me in the bakery and devotedly bows down before you—for all of this, we ask your holy prayers and blessings.

Wretched Herman.

22 May 1795[67]

As far as the search for "the settlement of Novgorodians" is concerned, the board of the Russian-American Company (RAC) repeatedly organized expeditions to the north. In January 1818, Colonial Chief Manager Ludwig (Leontii Adrianovich) von Hagemeister, departing on the next mission, wrote, "Tell Father Herman about the plan to the north and read him my suggestion to the office; perhaps he will provide good advice." But the legend remained a legend; "the settlement of Novogorodians" in Alaska was not found.

In the fall of 1795, Hieromonks Macarius and Juvenaly received a blessing from the archimandrite to undertake missionary work. On May 25, the first of them departed on the ship *Phoenix* for the Aleutian islands. Another passenger on this boat was O. A. Priashnishnikov, who carried communication to the Most-Holy Synod about the success of the mission.

> The other hieromonk, Juvenaly, was sent to the Iakutat Bay to convert the natives on the ship *The Three Saints* under the command of G. L. Pribilov. On board were twenty families of settlers and thirty families of *promyshlenniki* who were to build a settlement in Iakutat under the command of Polomoshnyi. Joseph himself and the manager Baranov decided to followed their route to Iakutat.
>
> However, Father Juvenaly did not make it to Iakutat. . . . Polomoshnyi, who didn't agree with Baranov about building a settlement in Iakutat, incited Pribilov, so that citing a lack of fresh water, he went down to Nunchek. From there, having filled his water barrels, he headed to Kodiak. Father Juvenaly remained in Nunchek.[68]

He spent the winter of 1795–1796 there in the redoubt of Saints Constantine and Helen.

By the summer of 1796, Father Juvenaly had already baptized 746 Chugach there. Archimandrite Joseph reported to the Most-Holy Synod that 6,746 people had been baptized in America in 1796. In the summer of 1796, Father Juvenaly conducted missionary work among the Kenai Indians on the Kenai Peninsula; then he moved into the interior regions of Alaska. There is evidence that he was able to reach the Kuskokwim Bay, where he was killed by Eskimos in the village of Kvingagak (currently known as Kuinegnak).

Having gathered information about Father Juvenaly's death forty years later, St Innocent (Veniaminov) wrote,

The reason for his death, they say, was only that from the very start he ordered the natives who were being baptized to give up polygamy. The local chiefs and important people, at the insistence of Father Juvenaly, went so far as to give up their children to be educated in Kodiak. But when Father Juvenaly departed from them, the natives regretted their decision and immediately chased after him, and, when they reached him, they attacked him.

They say that Father Juvenaly . . . had no concern to defend himself or to run away, which he could have easily done, particularly because he had a gun with him. But without any resistance he gave himself over to their hands and only asked mercy for his companions, which they did. After a long time, as the Americans themselves tell it, Father Juvenaly, who was already dead, arose and went after his murderers, saying something to them. The natives, thinking that he was alive, fell on him again and beat him. This scene was repeated several times. Finally, in order to rid themselves of him completely, the natives cut him up into pieces. It was only this that silenced the zealous preacher and, it can be said, the martyr for the Word of God. Yet the power of his words were not silenced: on that very place where the remains of the preacher lay, they

say that a column of smoke which extended to heaven immediately arose.[69]

This describes the martyric end of one of the missionaries, whose blood bore witness to the preaching of Christianity in America.

The missionary activity of Father Macarius, who was
accompanied by one of the novices, was very successful.
The Aleuts had already been in contact with Russians for
more than fifty years and many of them had been baptized by laymen. St Innocent noted, "Father Macarius
traveled from place to place and, when heading out for
distant settlements, did not have anyone with him for his
protection, except for one Russian as an assistant. The
very same Aleuts whom he was to baptize ferried him
around, fed him, and protected him."[70] On the Aleutian
island, he baptized "everyone without exception—2,472
people in all."

While on Unalaska Island, Father Macarius was
dragged into a struggle between Golikov and Shelikhov's
trading company and the company run by the Kiselev
brothers whose ship *Saints Zosima and Savatii* was at the
island in 1793. In 1792, *Saint Michael*, a ship of the Golikov
and Shelikov company, had been at the island; in 1794,
another Golikov–Shelikov company vessel, *Saints Simeon
and Anna*, arrived with a translator, Basil Peterovich
Merkul'ev, who was the director of the artel[71] of Russian
promyshlenniki. The Aleuts endured "terrible calamities"

from representatives of the Golikov–Shelikhov company. They forced the Aleuts to work the fur trade during the season of laying in stores for the winter; by this, they condemned them to starvation in the coming winter. They put women and children to work without pay; they forcibly took young Aleuts as concubines. They even committed a civil crime: they did not allow the Aleut *toion,*[72] Ivan Golotov, to stamp the furs that had been prepared in exchange for the tribute to the state; instead, they claimed the furs as their personal property.

Merkul'ev simply scoffed at the representatives of the Kiselev brothers' company. He took payment for the artel's delivery of the Kiselev workers to the Pribilof Islands but forbade them to hunt for marine animals there, announcing that those islands belonged to Shelikhov. Merkul'ev declared that all the Aleuts on Unalaska were employees of his [Golikov–Shelikhov's] company and forbade them to sell products to representatives of the Kiselev brothers' company. It is understandable that the Aleuts would take any opportunity to switch from service in the Golikov–Shelikhov company to the Kiselev brothers' company.

When Father Macarius arrived on Unalaska, Merkul'ev began to treat him as an employee of his company, as Golikov and Shelikhov had asked the synod to send an Orthodox mission to America. It is clear that Father Macarius had different ideas of Christian charity than Merkul'ev, so he took the side of the oppressed, the Aleuts, and the employees of the Kiselev brothers' company. The conflict became so inflamed that people associated with Merkul'ev even tried to kill Father Macarius.[73]

In the summer of 1796, Hieromonk Macarius, accompanied by several Aleuts, left for Russia on a ship of the Kiselev brothers to report to the Most-Holy Synod about the activity of the mission in America.

LIFE AND ASCETIC LABORS
OF THE MISSIONARIES

In the fall of 1795, the monks gathered the first crops from their garden. The harvest yielded only potatoes, radishes, and turnips. In subsequent years, experience showed that rutabaga, beets, garlic, and barley could also be grown on Kodiak. "We made flour from potatoes and pickled the turnips after cutting them into small pieces—we made up for the lack of salt with sea water and used the turnips throughout the entire winter and summer instead of cabbage. With the surplus remaining from our labors we helped poor locals and, by having a kind approach as is required of proselytizers, we created a good opinion of us in the minds of the Americans."[74]

In 1796, the construction of Holy Resurrection Church was completed. Meanwhile, in Russia the decision had been made to send a bishop to America "because a hierarch located there, in the event that they kill priests, could ordain others from among the very same natives, of whom many have already learned both the Russian language and Holy Scripture and therefore could both more quickly and convincingly explain it to their compatriots in their own tongue and attract them to Holy Baptism."[75] The translator O. A. Priashnishnikov delivered the news to Kodiak that Father Joseph had been called to Irkutsk to be consecrated a bishop. He had returned from Russia in the middle of October 1797 on the *Feniks*, under the command of the naval navigator corps lieutenant Gabriel Terent'evich Talin. In St Petersburg, Priashnishnikov had been removed from the merchant class and assigned to the Kodiak mission at the rank of a collegiate translator, which corresponded with the rank of an officer.

Archimandrite Joseph left Kodiak in June 1798 on the vessel *Feniks*; Hierodeacon Stephen and novice Dmitry Avdeev traveled with him. In Irkutsk, Father Joseph was consecrated bishop of Kodiak and America, with an appointment to the Irkutsk Vicariate on Kodiak.[76]

Bishop Joseph returned to America in 1799 on the same ship *Feniks*. Father Macarius, Father Stephen, novice Dmitry Avdeev, several married priests, and other clergymen traveled along with him. They all perished in a shipwreck. The *Feniks* did not return to America; the site of the wreck is not known. The novice Nikita Semonov also drowned. This happened sometime during his stay in America; the year is not known. In 1811, the vicariate on Kodiak was abolished.

After this, the correspondence between Father Herman and the Valaam brotherhood was interrupted. It usually took a whole year for mail travel from Okhotsk to St Petersburg. Owing to a series of shipwrecks, from 1798 until 1802 no ships reached Kodiak from Russia.

Meanwhile in Russia, Metropolitan Ambrose replaced Metropolitan Gabriel in 1799, and in 1801 Valaam's superior, Hegumen Nazarius, went into retirement, so that Father Herman's letters to Valaam were left without a reply.

In this way, by 1798 in America there remained Hieromonk Athanasius (age forty), Hierodeacon Nectarios (age twenty-nine), and the monks Herman (age forty-seven) and Joseph (age twenty-nine). They undertook no missionary journeys and focused all their activity on the inhabitants of Kodiak and the surrounding regions. Father Athanasius became the formal head of the mission, but Father Nectarios actually directed all the activity of the monks. As before, he taught in the school. Father Herman directed the agricultural work of the mission, and Father Joseph was his assistant.

During this time, important changes occurred in Russia that affected Russian America. In 1795, Shelikhov died. The new Emperor Paul I came to the throne in 1796. On the basis of Shelikhov's company, the Russian-American Company [RAC] was founded in 1799, and given a monopoly. Baranov remained the chief manager of the RAC in Alaska. From there, he continued the expansion of the company's activity along the Alaskan coast to the east and, in the early 1800s, into California and the Hawaiian Islands.

The RAC subjected the native population of Alaska to extremely cruel exploitation. Hieromonk Gideon wrote in his diary,

In 1801 the company drove the Aleuts in the Sitkhinok expedition [to hunt] for beaver in the following manner: Having put stocks on their feet and collars on their necks, having made birch rods for the youth, whips for the thirty-year-olds and cudgels for the elderly, the boat was sent out with a cannon and guns.

The Russian *promyshlenniki* stood at attention with loaded guns on the western cape of Kodiak at the exit to the shore saying, "Well! If you do not go on the expedition, let's say (while cocking their triggers), we will start to shoot." Under this pressure who can display their displeasure? When they arrived at Sitkhinok, they fired the cannon. Standing with loaded guns, they set out the birch rods, whips, cudgels, stocks, and collars along the village, saying, "Whoever doesn't want to go on the expedition, let him choose for himself from these." At that time someone began to make excuses. They suddenly grabbed him, bound him in iron shackles, and condemned him until he wheezed and could barely say, "I'll go."

In that same year in the first days of May, one of the elders, who had been selected for a bird hunting expedition, was sent out in such poor shape that, having not been able to crawl a hundred *sazhens*[77] to the place they were spending the night, he slept on the beach with his wife. In the morning he was summoned or, more accurately, was carried to attest to his illness to the governing house [most likely, to Baranov]. There he was told, "Although you cannot walk, you can keep watch so that dogs do not eat the boat." . . . Due to the burdensome company workers described above, the Aleuts endured a great famine in all the settlements in the wintertime. They eat the seal bladders, in which they keep fat and sour salmon caviar, walrus hides, and other things made in the settlement due to the lack of mussels and seaweed at times when the shallow cove is covered in ice. A compassionate person can hardly hold back tears while seeing these unfortunate people in such a condition, that they more closely resemble corpses than living beings. After the departure of the men on an expedition, those left in the settlements are women with young children and the withered old men and women. Due to the lack of *baidarkas* as well as the quit-rents imposed on them by the company involving cleaning fish, digging daylilies,[78] and gathering berries in the summer, they do not have the time to put up stores for themselves of the necessary food for the winter and therefore it often happens that many die of hunger.

Is not all of this more aggravating and more ruinous than the tribute that has not been collected since 1794? Is this a sign of kind and friendly relations? The words "kind and friendly relations" are always foremost on the lips and the statements of the company, but not in their deeds.[79]

This document makes clear why, thirty years later, another chief manager of Russian America, Baron Ferdinand P. Wrangell,[80] without irony called the rule of Baranov and his companions "despotism by a gang of robbers."

The natives only found sympathy and support from their spiritual leaders. Father Herman was the main defender of the Kodiak Aleuts. Wrangell wrote, "Having a fiery temperament, he was not indifferent to the offenses and oppressions which other members of the mission frequently experienced from the local authorities and with fervor stood up for the natives' rights, which were being violated by the obstinacy, cruelty, and debauchery of the *promyshlenniki* and management. And because of this, he himself was subject to a multitude of discomforts."[81]

Baranov's letter of July 24, 1800, to E. G. Larionov states,

> The multiplicity of leadership and dis-leadership which are spread here by the remaining monks, translator, and hired seafarer are noticeably upsetting; I have simply not been able to make peace with them. . . . Through visitors, each of whom they question, they know and judge and settle every step of the *baidarshchiki* [leaders of the artel] and of the *promyshlenniki*. They always take things at their worst; they spread threats of future consequences everywhere.
>
> The most caustic of the hermits has particularly intruded upon us. He is not to be compared with Marakii; he is called

Herman—a hack writer and a chatterer. Although he does not
leave his seclusion for anyone nor for Church, avoiding the
temptations of the world, he penetrates everywhere into not
only the daily but the nightly activities and thoughts of each
one of us.[82]

Relations between the monks and Baranov continued to worsen. This period of activities of the mission is
described in detail in Hieromonk Gideon's letter of June
2, 1805, to Metropolitan Ambrose of St Petersburg and
Novgorod:

Your most magnanimous Metropolitan!

After receiving reliable news of the unfortunate wreck of
the company's ship *Feniks,* on which His Grace Bishop Joseph
of Kodiak was sailing from Okhotsk, the following is what has
occurred with the monastics remaining here.

In addition to suggesting to the Aleuts a multitude of
reproachful nonsense, which could only have been thought up
by the company to disgrace the honor of the clergy, the chief
manager Baranov, out of jealousy to the great love of this innocent people to their enlighteners and considering this to be a
belittling of his authority over the Americans who have been
worn out by various work and company taxes, sent a letter on
July 14, 1800, to the *eikonom*[83] of the spiritual mission, monk
Herman. In it he forbade the clergy to interact with the Americans and ordered to drive away all those who show kindness
to their preachers out of gratitude.

Despite the imperial decree, issued in 1796, the Kodiak people still had not been administered the oath of loyalty to the Russian Throne, since they were being dispatched far from the company and due to other time constraints. On January 1, 1801, Hieromonk Athanasius asked Baranov's permission to do this, for which the same hieromonk was cursed, driven away, and forbidden to return.

Then about twenty people from various villages including their *toions* assembled to ask Baranov if he would relieve them of further hunting trips with the Sitkhinok crew, promising instead to hunt around their villages, but they were driven off with harsh threats and even ordered to all be ready for hunts by spring. Being immeasurably distressed, they dared in their despair to tell the spiritual mission that as a result they did not want to go with that crew [on a hunt] because many of their relatives died there and other villages had become deserted; and, if Baranov killed them for this, then they brought new parkas with them, and they asked the clergy that they bury them afterward in these new parkas and be witnesses to their innocent murder.

Seeing this, the clergy and the others gathered—the master officer, the navigator Talin, and the translator of the spiritual mission, Priashnishnikov—all being in horror at what they were hearing, they tried to convince them to endure all these difficult events with long suffering and, moreover, assured them of the mercy of the Lord on High. Having barely calmed them down, they offered the oath of loyalty to the sovereign, to which they readily agreed and promised to be obedient in all things.

Therefore, accompanied by those officers to the church, they were sworn in by Hieromonk Athanasius. Upon leaving the church, when they had just begun to get into their *baidarkas*,[84] the assistant of the manager Baranov, Kuskov with his *promyshlenniki*, seizing one of them, a *toion* they knew, took him to the company barracks and, having fettered him in irons, imprisoned him in a dark storeroom, where not only the windows, but even the chinks were sealed up. They even went after the others with weapons in a *baidarka* but did not catch anyone.

After this incident Baranov wanted to imprison another *toion* whom he had taken captive; he was the godson of a bishop, who had come as a friend to visit the clergy. Having learned of this, they thought to let him out at night, but, being concerned, Hieromonk Athanasius ordered that first his *baidarka* be carried out. He went to it and wanted to only travel a short distance; suddenly the *promyshlenniki* stopped the *baidarka,* and, at the orders of manager Baranov, seized the hieromonk. Baranov himself began to curse with the greatest vehemence, calling him a runaway servant of the Lord, while calling all the monks and the two officers mentioned above rebels.

During this unpleasant event, the monk Herman asked Baranov to honestly state, without any cursing, the cause of his dissatisfaction. The manager replied with a shout: "Indeed! You found some kind of an oath and corrupted all the Americans."

The humble elder replied, "The imperial decree was issued to everyone; and if what the spiritual mission has done is unlawful, then it would be better to submit it to the government, where everything can be examined lawfully."

But Baranov, not heeding him, shouted, "What is the decree to you? What is a court to you?" And in a most extreme fit of rage he made various threats: that no one could visit him [St Herman—Trans.] and that they [the monks—Trans.] could not even go anywhere. And so everyone was terribly afraid and simply expected that the *promyshlenniki*, at Baranov's command, would either drag him off somewhere or start to beat him. We were barely brave enough to walk from the shore to our house, around which for some time we saw *promyshlenniki* with guns. It is for this reason that we did not dare to go out freely, even to church, and, what is more, we conducted all our church services in our house for more than a year, and all due to doubting our loyalty, because of the prohibition of the oath.

When the time came to gather an expedition to hunt for beaver, then Kuskov armed the *baidarka* not only with guns, but also with a cannon. He went to the settlements to those who had been brought for the oath. For greater glory a member of the expedition, Kandakov, was ordered to travel in front, approaching with obscene cursing and various mockeries in reproach of the monastics. He shouted loudly, "Attention! The popes are coming with Osip (this was the name of the translator) to bring you to take an oath!" And when they brought the rudder of the *baidarka* to the shore, at that time they all shouted, "Here is your cross—venerate it!" It is shameful to even recall the kind of animosity, violence, and excess to which they submitted the islanders.[85]

It is to be expected that Baranov's interpretation of these events would be different. This is how he described what happened:

On the next, on New Year's Day, something new again happened. After the liturgy, the steward and the sailor Herr Podtgazh along with several *promyshlenniki* were drinking tea with me. Suddenly the hieromonk ran in, all worked up, and spiritedly called out that this year no one should be appointed or sent on the bird hunting expedition and that the entire population of the island should at once be brought to them for the oath.

For my part, having given him tea, I said that . . . it is not the time to gather the people for the oath, since we do not have enough provisions in storage . . . and since it is inconvenient for the islanders to travel to us in the current frigid winter and rough weather. . . .

Right then and there he called me a traitor to the Emperor, since I did not allow the oath. It made me feel vexed to hear such a thing . . . for all my zeal for the benefit of the fatherland and for the glory of the monarchy. . . .

He called me out, saying that those who openly keep a woman and have children should not be allowed in church according to the Spiritual Regulation. And although I certainly know that this cannot be in that Regulation, which was published by our wise Emperor,[86] yet in order that they in their anger not have anything to curse at in God's House, I stopped attending [church] after the New Year's.[87]

This letter reveals all the craftiness of Baranov. He reproaches Hieromonk Athanasius about the refreshments, besides which he makes himself out to be an expert on the Spiritual Regulation and seemingly quoting the opinion of the emperor, while completely misconstruing what has happened.

The historian A. V. Grinev has made a thorough analysis of the relationship between the monks and the manager Baranov in this period:

> In their reports to the synod the monks complained that Baranov, "having burdened the entire population of both sexes with infinite difficulties in working for his company, none less out of envy of the people's great love to us, he formed an intense hatred for us since their love undermined his great power and command over them." This hatred was directed most of all at the monk Herman. . . . Father Herman particularly actively fought for the interests of the enslaved natives. The documents state that he, "a simple monk, showed himself to be an almost perfect Russian Las Casas,[88] but his zeal was entirely without success, since the law of the mighty could not be swayed in this case by the convictions of truth."[89]

Subsequently, the situation of the missionaries only grew worse.

In 1802 on the Bright Pascha[90] a drunk *promyshlennik*, Chernov, was sent by Baranov and with great rudeness ordered Hierodeacon Nectarios to unlock the bell tower. The hierodeacon did not want to give them the key, since the church was locked with only one lock, and the big bell was broken. But the above-mentioned *promyshlennik* vigorously threatened to drag him by force or to break the bell tower window. Meanwhile, due to his illness, the translator, Prianishnikov, requested by note that the hieromonk and hierodeacon make the sign of the Holy Cross over his home. When they had just barely arrived [to the home of Prianishnikov], Baranov and his *promyshlenniki* ran up and in a most fiery anger indecently shouted, cursed, and threatened the hieromonk—to put him in a *baidarka* and send him to some unknown place. Grabbing the hierodeacon by the chest with great vigor, he wanted to hang the hierodeacon from the bell tower. Throughout all of this boldness, the *promyshlenniki*, hoping in their manager, were saying, "It is a long way up to God; it is a long way away to the tsar; just let our manager be healthy."[91]

Of the other figures active in this conflict, the navigator Talin was sent to Russia at the end of 1802; he retired and became a novice at Valaam Monastery. The translator Prianishnikov was seriously ill and probably died in 1802. It is known for certain that in 1804 the monks no longer had a translator.

From January 1801 through the middle of September 1802, the monks were practically incarcerated; they could not even go to church. It was only the arrival at Kodiak of the crew of the galiot *Saint Alexander Nevskii* on September 13, 1802, that eased the circumstances.

Father Gideon wrote, "Concerned that due to rejecting the oath and the repression of the clergy there would be denunciations from the company officers who had arrived on the ship, the manager tried to smooth over his actions and therefore found himself bound to send the manifest and envelopes which belonged to the spiritual mission and which had been retained. We began to hold divine services in the church on September 15, 1802."[92]

Baranov was a man of his time. The historian A. V. Grinev noted,

> He was by no means a defender of human rights and personal freedom: the order, which reigned in Russian and her colonies, fit him well. Expanding and strengthening to the best of his ability Russian holdings in the New World, Baranov frequently did not spare himself or others in acting in accordance with the principle "the people for the empire, and not the empire for the people." Similar conceptions of patriotism were broadly characteristic of Russian society, and Baranov was a great patriot. The labor, health, and, now and then, the life of certain individuals and a whole generation of native and Russian employees of the Russian American Company were brought by him as a sacrifice to the government.[93]

In the spring of 1803, G. T. Talin received a letter, written by the monks of Kodiak mission on July 31, 1802, and sent to the Most-Holy Synod. This was the first correspondence from the missionaries in America since

1798, since from that time no ship had left Kodiak for Russia. The letter had the effect of a bolt of lightning in a clear sky. The missionaries reported on the multitude of repressions of the Aleuts by Baranov and his assistants; it also told of the impossibility of carrying out missionary work in such circumstances. But most important, the members of the Most-Holy Synod learned with surprise that Bishop Joseph and his retinue had perished in 1799 in a shipwreck. It had seemed in St Petersburg that the Kodiak mission was, if not flourishing, as least successfully developing.

It also became clear that the employees of the RAC in St Petersburg had taken the money that had been assigned by the government to support the mission. A. N. L'vov wrote, "Arguments arose over the money, which had been released for the Kodiak bishop's residence. The Company had received these funds for four years (from 1800 to 1803) and did not want to return them to the synod, or to the treasury, explaining its refusal on the grounds that almost the entire sixteen thousand had been spent on supporting the four monks who were on Kodiak, although the Company had earlier promised to support them at their own expense."[94] It should be noted that in Russia for the support of a monastic in a bishop's residence, twenty-four rubles a year was paid for a hieromonk and twenty a year for a monk. The comparison of these sums speaks for itself. It is clear that the directors of the company simply did not want to return the money they had stolen.

Then the Most-Holy Synod offered the board of the RAC in St Petersburg to send a new bishop to America. This time the board of the RAC treated the offer of the synod with caution. A company with a total monopoly on the exploitation of the natural wealth of Alaska had already been created, and it had no particular enthusiasm for the enlightenment of natives. The board of the RAC replied, "It is not yet time there for a resident bishop, who would be assigned solely for the ordination of local natives to clerical orders, since as yet a central place for assembly has not been designated, where the settlements of the company would be supplied with a good climate and top soil for agriculture and other enterprises."[95]

To better understand the state of affairs there, the Most-Holy Synod sent Hieromonk Gideon (Gabriel Fedotov) of the St Alexander Nevsky Monastery to America to inspect the activity of the mission. On behalf of the RAC, the colony was to be inspected by a Chamberlain of the Court, Nicholas Peterovich Rezanov—the son-in-law of Shelikhov. In the instructions, which Father Gideon received before his departure for America, he was directed "to not interfere in any way in secular affairs and matters." Father Gideon and Rezanov departed for America in 1803 on vessels in the first Russian around-the-world expedition; Father Gideon, on the *Neva,* which was commanded by Iu. F. Lisianskii, and Rezanov, on the *Nadezhda,* whose captain was I. F. Kruzenshtern. It turned out that Father Gideon and Captain Lisianskii represented opposing interests. Father Gideon was to defend the interests of the missionaries, and Lisianskii, those of the RAC. The company had paid for half of the cost to outfit the expedition, and the main task of the *Neva* was to obtain company goods in Russian America and then travel to China to sell furs. In reality, Lisianskii was an employee of the RAC during the expedition.

During the voyage, Father Gideon was subjected to various attacks and pressure from the captain of the vessel. He wrote,

> Captain Lisianskii and midshipman Berkh are people of a restless disposition. They caused me many insults, for which my antidote was abundant patience. I overlook in silence the repeated prohibition to serve divine services on Sundays and feasts of the Lord, which at sea [are] the sole comfort of those who know God. I am ashamed to recall the various caustic gibes about religion. The son of archpriest Lisianskii from Nizhin, it seems, having been born and raised in the very cradle of religion, often had the desire to drink Tenerife[96] wine while saying the following to me, "Father! To the health of the Mother of God."[97]

During the voyage, Father Gideon received the following instructions from Rezanov:

> Appealing with particular respect to your apostolic calling, which you have so zealously taken upon yourself, I am sure that upon arrival in America you will fulfill in the best possible

way the royal will of our most gracious sovereign, who is attending to the dissemination of the Orthodox Christian faith for the personal well-being of the American people, so that, cleaning their minds from prejudices, you will plant in their hearts the rule of the true worship of God and that, driving away by humble means all superstition, which is intolerable to true religion, you will prepare them for society, show them their obligations in their relationship to the sovereign and their neighbors, and make them good sons of Russia. Success in this important transformation promises eternal glory, the goodwill of the sovereign, and the gratitude of future generations.

After your arrival in America try, through gentle comportment, to gain the affection of the local authorities and all the residents, assist the former through all measures to establish good harmony between the Russians and the Americans, and instill in both groups that now they both comprise one Russian nation, and that they are both sons of one sovereign. . . .

Your Reverence is aware that in these happy days of ours, the education of Russia is the primary interest of its philanthropic ruler. In accordance with this lofty intent, I charge you to take the Kodiak school under your particular care and to make it a proper academic institution, to which end, by my orders to the Kodiak authorities, you will receive all the assistance that they can provide. If the youth there has already learned grammar, then give them a true understanding of the Law of God and natural law, devoting time, meanwhile, to show them the rules of spelling and arithmetic, and to establish the introductory principles of the other sciences.

Though planting crops, animal husbandry, and other agricultural activities do not belong to Your Reverence's field, still
I, as an enlightened man, most humbly request that, if you
have knowledge in any of these subjects, then do not deprive
the local authority of your advice and contribute to the common good and welfare of the region.[98]

Hieromonk Gideon arrived on Kodiak in June 1804
and took charge of the mission. Immediately after his
arrival, Father Gideon undertook a two-month missionary voyage by *baidarka* to the Kodiak settlements, during which he baptized 528 people and served thirty-eight
marriages. During this trip, he almost drowned when the
baidarka sank in the bay between Kodiak and Aiakhtalik
Islands.

One of the first duties of Father Gideon on Kodiak
was to revive the operations of the school. The school,
founded by Archimandrite Joseph, continued through
the end of 1800; Father Nectarios had taught in it. Then
Baranov dismissed the monks from teaching in the school
and assigned the *promyshlennik* Iudin to be the teacher. In
March 1805, the school was opened again, with the participants—about sixty students—divided into two classes.
The students were taught the short catechism, Biblical
history, reading, writing, and arithmetic.

Beside that, the Kodiak Aleut pupils were taught
farming skills: planting, weeding, and harvesting vegetables. The teaching of gardening began in the spring

and finished in the fall, so that the participants were present for the planting of vegetables as well as the gathering of the harvest. In August, the school held public exams, and Rezanov gave awards to the outstanding students. Then Father Gideon tried to interest the *promyshlennik* Borisov in teaching mathematics at the school but was sharply rebuffed by Baranov's assistant, Ivan Ivanovich Banner. He curtly reminded Father Gideon that he had no right to interfere in secular matters and, reproaching him for insubordination, threatened troubles with the authorities.

Father Gideon described the life of the monks in 1805:

The clerics live in one house, which was given by the company, in a tight place between the manager's house and the general company *bania*.[99] Most of their subsistence comes from their own labors; besides keeping a garden, they gather berries and mushrooms, catch fish, and receive a portion from the company. All these sort of labors are carried out with the assistance of the very kind Americans, whom the company tried with all their efforts to drive away. The clergy wear clothes and shoes left over from the property of His Grace Bishop Joseph. . . .

Hieromonk [Athanasius] . . . and monk Herman . . . are lovers of solitude; they have the desire to stay in America, but they thoroughly miss the life in a hermitage, due to the location of their house right next to laity, in which it is not possible for them to avoid rumors, excessive temptations, and the inhuman behavior caused by the Russians, in part amongst themselves, but primarily with the Americans; they also lament the distance needed to get firewood and other necessities for their home and the inadequacies and congestion of that place. Their plan is to move away some distance from all that bustle and make themselves a quiet habitation, which is particularly close to church. If there will be no help from anywhere, that is, neither officially nor from someone in particular, and if it will not be possible to pay for their sustenance and have some financial support for all the things that they need, then they will rely on their own strength and select a suitable place to build, one that is near the forest, near a river, for the preparation of fish, and suited for developing gardens.[100]

The general condition of the colony at this time was grave. The German researcher G. I. Langsdorf, who visited Russian America in 1805–1806, noted,

The great old age of Baranov [in 1806, he was 60 years old], the unconscionable behavior of his assistants and their terrible management, the size of the settlement and enormity of the distance between them and the main office in St Petersburg, the inadequacy of necessary supervision and justice—these, I am convinced, are the main reasons for much mistreatment, against which it is impossible for one man—even the most honest of men—to fight. The management in each separate village is purely despotic. The leaders of the Kodiak office do whatever they want, making no reports to anyone and not being subject to any supervision.[101]

Having visited New Arkhangel'sk, the Lutheran Langsdorf was truly amazed after observing the burial of Russian *promyshlenniki*. No one accompanied them on their final journey, no one read prayers, and crosses were not placed over their graves. The authorities simply ordered the Aleuts to carry the body of the departed to the cemetery and to bury it in the ground. Assuming that his readers could not believe that this happened in fact, he wrote, "All of this must seem exaggeration and unbelievable. . . . I cannot comprehend such behavior. All the more, what could motivate me to make up such unpleasant stories? I would prefer to share comforting and pleasant fact with my readers!"[102]

It is also necessary to note that, after Archimandrite Joseph left Kodiak in the summer of 1798, there was no harmony among the remaining missionaries. Some of them could not resist worldly temptations. As has already been mentioned, because of Baranov's resistance the missionary activity among the Kodiak Aleuts had largely been suspended before the arrival of Father Gideon in 1804. The seafarer G. I. Davidov noted that the baptized Kodiak Aleuts

are ceasing to be Christians. Whenever it comes into their minds, they now abandon wives, just as they did before. And they have not the slightest respect for the images printed on paper that are given out to them; I myself have seen these icons wrapped around tobacco. In truth, when they are around

Russians, they try to act as if they know several rituals, such as how to cross themselves before the start of any work, but due to their uncertain understanding, they sometime cross themselves before the start of such activities that among Christians would be considered sinful.

Those Koniag [Kodiak Aleuts] whom the priests have taken in to raise from childhood, having learned to read and write, are the only ones to receive a proper understanding of the Christian law from the daily example. . . .

Moreover, the lack of respect to the priests, some of whom—though not all—are thoroughly distinguished people, and the general depravity of the Russians, are not strong examples to prompt the natives to abandon their superstitions.[103]

In 1806, Father Nectarios voluntarily left Kodiak on the brig *Saint Mariia Magdalina* under the command of lieutenant A. V. Mashin and went to Russia. He had always suffered from poor health. He was headed for St Petersburg but did not reach the capital. Father Nectarios reposed on December 11, 1808, and was buried in the village of Gonba in the Mamlyshskii Deanery of the Viatsk Diocese.[104]

As has been noted, some *promyshlenniki* left wives in Russia, and therefore marriages between Russians and local natives occurred only if the groom, in the presence of several witnesses, confirmed that he had no wife in Russia.

This is an example of how that occurred:

> On this tenth day of January 1800 on Kodiak Island in the Pav-lovskaia Harbor, before the American Ecclesiastical Retinue, a *promyshlennik* from the city Irkutsk, the settlement Ziminsk, the peasant Nikifor, son of Efim Zakharov, gave this pledge, that I, Zakharov, have no wife in Russia. I swear to this before God, and if I will be convicted of this [bigamy], then I subject myself to civil court and severe punishment.
>
>   Therefore I wish to be joined in lawful marriage to the recently baptized American from the Izaksk settlement, Naa-pii, in baptism Pelagia, to which I confirm by my signature and the undersigned witnesses.
>
>   Nikifor Zakharov.
>
>   At the request of Peter Kazaritin, I, Timothy Tarakanov, sign this as his witness.
>
>   I, Andrew Otolin, bear witness.[105]

However, after Rezanov's arrival at Kodiak in March 1805, he forbade marriages between Russians and natives in general, unless the Russians expressed a desire to stay in America forever.

Since he had no authority to regulate marriage, this decree did not remain in force for long. In 1805, there were a few more than thirty Russian–aboriginal families who intended to stay in America. However, practically all the Russians, who by this time numbered more than 300 people, had concubines among the local natives. In part, this can be explained by the fact that in Kamchatka, from where a significant portion of the Russians came, for every thirty Russian men there was only one Russian woman. Therefore on Kodiak at the start of the nineteenth century there was a large quantity of illegitimate children. In the summer of 1806, Rezanov left America and from that time on, Russian–aboriginal marriages were once again officially registered.

In April 1807, the school held annual exams. The best students were Paramon Chumovitskii, Alexi Kotel'nikov, Ivan Kad'iakskii,[106] and Christopher Prianishnikov. All of them were given monetary prizes for outstanding studies.

FATHER HERMAN TAKES CHARGE
OF THE KODIAK MISSION

In time, Father Herman established good relations with Baranov. Langsdorf wrote that "a long life spent among natives, daily interaction with scoundrels, a lack of people who were worthy of trust, and a conviction in the necessity of strict and severe measures both for personal safety and for the benefit of the company—all of this deadened compassionate feelings in him and made him inflexible."[107] As a true Christian, Father Herman loved and forgave everyone. The entire population of Pavlovskaia Harbor also loved and respected Father Herman; children especially loved him. As soon as Father Herman appeared on the street, children would run to him from all directions and ask him to tell a fairy tale or some kind of story. Father Herman knew few fairy tales, but he did know the lives of the saints well, which he told the children with such touching simplicity and freshness that the children did not need any fairy tales.

P. Chumovitskii became the translator for the mission. With his help, Father Gideon translated into Aleut the Lord's Prayer, which was sung in church even after his departure.

In 1807, Hieromonk Gideon left for Kamchatka for an inspection of the churches there; after that, in 1809, he arrived in St Petersburg. He decided to appoint Father Herman as the head of the mission on Kodiak. Informing Baranov of this appointment, Father Gideon wrote him in a May 17, 1807, letter:

> The late bishop entrusted the entire house, property, and finances to the supervision of monk Herman. Likewise, the clergy remaining here were assigned to his care. He was ordered to treat them as he best saw fit, to decisively deny them their whims, and to particularly predispose everyone to his will, in accordance with the circumstances that may arise.
>
> For these reasons I also, at my departure for St Petersburg, regarding with particular esteem the great virtues and rare qualities of mind and heart of this educated, experienced, hard-working, and most-honorable father, have complete trust that due to his zealousness, attentiveness, and insight nothing will be missed.

With resolve and complete satisfaction, I assign leadership of this spiritual mission to him. I pray that you, sir, in what belongs to the spiritual sphere, may concern yourself with him and provide him all possible assistance in the prevention of any sort of unfortunate circumstance that may arise.

I intend, as is my responsibility, to inform the preeminent member of the Most-Holy governing Synod, His Eminence the metropolitan, the honored Ambrose about my impartial selection; and moreover, I earnestly admit to you, that in this selection I am comforted and reassured by the fact that I very often had the pleasure of hearing your Honor greatly praise this peace-loving elder who is overflowing with meekness, calmness, and humble wisdom. . . . This praise is more important for him than any other praise.[108]

Hieromonk Gideon left detailed instructions for Father Hermann in a note dated June 11, 1807:

Reverend Father Herman!

Departing now for St Petersburg to carry out my duties, I deemed it absolutely necessary to charge you with the leadership of the American-Kodiak spiritual mission, about which I have already informed his Honor, the collegiate counselor and chief manager of this region, Alexander Andreevich Baranov. I consider it both the best arrangement and my obligation to set forth my thoughts, beyond our private discussions, in a letter to you.

1. Knowing your virtues and practical zeal for the betterment of this region, I am sustained by the gratifying hope that you will not neglect to inculcate in the hearts of the Russians and Americans the rules of piety, Christian charity, and friendly ties among both groups using your well-tested exhortations. You know that the first responsibility of clergy is to give an example of Christian sanctity in their own lives; I do not doubt but that you will properly guide them in this way. The particular task before your Reverence is to see that everyone, in whatever responsibility he has, carries it out in a conscientious, honest, and God-pleasing manner.

2. There are a great many leaks throughout the entire church here, about which I have already informed the Kodiak office; so it is your responsibility to now insist on its being reroofed. Vestments, sacred vessels, and books are essential to conduct divine services; it is up to you to assign supervision to either Hieromonk Athanasius or monk Joseph and to take particular care for the conscientious preservation of all these things.

3. Upon my arrival I noted with pleasure your uncommon restraint in finances and exemplary management, such as your reliable means of preserving bread . . . just as with other property, I am entirely sure that in your zeal you will do all that can be done in such matters. . . .

4. After my arrival on the *Neva* to this wild and remote region, my entire being trembled with fear at the initial sight of both the harsh climate and the barren coarseness of the land. But when I saw the hard-earned fruits from your enthusiastic

efforts applied to your good-natured relationship with the Americans, as well as in the agriculture and farming they have done, then this unexpected sight filled my soul with a pleasant calm. And, after his arrival, even His Honor [Rezanov] gazed with a similar satisfaction on these accomplishments of yours in this wild-looking country. For their even greater encouragement, in your presence, he personally rewarded those Americans you had nurtured for their industrious obedience to you. Then, for the development of this region, he deemed it best to place three principal elements at the foundation: 1—agriculture, 2—education, 3—population growth. He also asked me that everyone apply their minds to these principles, so as to more rapidly enrich this region.

5. So for my part, at my departure I remind you to be even more attentive to this, since the beginnings have already been laid; I consider it unnecessary to explain the details, inasmuch as you are sufficiently experienced in this. You can obtain help in this from the company, about which His Grace has already instructed the office, and I have informed the Most-Honorable Alexander Andreevich Baranov.

6. It is with pleasure that I entrust particular care to Your Reverence for the Russian-American school that I have been managing. In the first group, the children must be taught reading, writing, and the short catechism; in the second group, grammar, arithmetic, sacred history, and civil history, as well as geography. In addition to the sciences, do not neglect subjects relating to agriculture; instead of taking

breaks, study how to prepare gardens, to plant and to sow vegetables, to weed, to gather important herbs and roots, and to catch fish.

The established order in the school must be maintained in the future; instructions from me have been left there. Ivan Kad'iakskii is the teacher; Christopher Prianishnikov, his colleague; and Alexi Kotel'nikov, their assistant. Paramon Chumovitskii, with the assistance of the others, has been charged with compiling a dictionary of the Aleutian language and a short outline of the grammar of that language. He should also be your translator. Likewise, maintain proper attention to and the diligence of the group of students who are farming. The company is responsible for supplying you with every means it has that is necessary for that. Most of all, be careful to fill their young hearts with the principles of faith, fear of God, and all morality; punish them for offenses. Your love for all that is good leaves me no doubt that you will carry out all of this in the best possible manner.

7. Your financial support, according to His Grace's assurance (as you are aware), has been placed in the care of the local manager, about which I, for my part, also asked him. For good order, your requests should be in your name only.

8. Most of all, try to keep peace, quiet, and harmony among the brotherhood. I hope that monk Joseph, as your spiritual son, will not scorn your instruction, although Hieromonk Athanasius, of course, will be difficult for you. . . . You, as an experienced and skillful spiritual doctor, will keep moderation

in all things. I, for my part, ask and pray the Almighty Giver of gifts that He send down upon you the strength so that you can do His goodwill and more.[109]

Reverend Father Herman!

I place my remaining books in your care, along with some other items. I ask you to keep them until my return.

Alexander Nevsky Lavra Cathedral, Hieromonk Gideon

1807, June 11

St Pavlovskaia Harbor[110]

Forsaking America, Father Gideon took with him one of the best students, the Creole Prokopii Lavrov. It was assumed that after an education in a theological seminary, he would return to Kodiak.

Lavrov received his education in the St Petersburg Theological Seminary and was ordained a priest. In 1810, he was sent across Siberia to America at the expense of the RAC. During this trip, he was subjected to great harassment from company employees. In the fall, he boarded the RAC's vessel, *Saint Mariia Magdalina*, which was to travel from Okhotsk to Kodiak. Owing to the poor condition of the ship, it could only reach Kamchatka, where it stayed for the winter. There Lavrov gave a report to the archbishop of Irkutsk, in which he asked him to let him to serve in the Irkutsk Diocese. He was granted permission, despite the fact that the Church gravely needed such a priest on Kodiak, because he was

only twenty-five years old and knew the language of the
Kodiak Aleuts. Lavrov initially served on Kamchatka
and then in Irkutsk.[111]

Father Gideon, while returning to Russia on the *Sitkha*,
visited the Aleutian Islands in July 1807. He baptized 141
children and married forty couples on Unalaska Island.
He recorded in his notes that the Aleuts "know and reverently observe all Church feasts, listen to the instructions
impressed upon them with extraordinary desire and love;
and fulfill these instructions in deed." At this time, there
was a chapel of St Nicholas on the neighboring island of
Umnak. It was built by the Aleuts under the direction of
toion Ivan Glotov. He led morning prayers in it himself
and read the hours on Sundays and feast days.

Father Gideon arrived in St Petersburg in 1809. He
was appointed deputy abbot of the St Alexander Nevsky
Lavra, and then was abbot of the Skovorodskii and
Iverskii Monasteries. In 1821, he went into retirement
at the Konevsky Monastery. In 1834, he moved to the
Andrusovskaia Nikolaevskaia Hermitage in the Olo-
netsk Diocese, where he died on November 1, 1843. He
was seventy-three.

This is how Father Herman came to head the Kodiak
mission starting in 1807. Monk Joseph and Hieromonk
Athanasius were subordinate to him. "This monk [Father
Herman] was the most worthy member of the mission.
He was distinguished from everyone by his piety and

intelligence and, in fact, led the mission, though he was a simple monk."[112]

After the departure of Father Gideon, the number of students in the school markedly decreased. Even in the spring of 1807, the company sent away about sixty students to do various jobs, because there was nothing to feed them. Father Herman was left with about twenty boys, whom he instructed in agriculture on Spruce Island. In the winter, he taught them reading, writing, the law of God, sacred history, and church singing. But even this number of students gradually shrunk, so that in 1811 the school had practically ceased to exist. The missionaries were left with only one translator—Paramon Chumovitskii, an Aleut from the village of Karluk—and a few boys, who were singers.

Despite the fact that the school did not operate for long, many Creoles received a primary education in it and subsequently worked for the RAC as shop assistants, bookkeepers, and directors of redoubts. For practically the first time, the school purposefully taught the local population the Russian language and farming skills. Following this, only a few children of Russian *promyshlenniki* studied in the school. Father Joseph taught them catechism; the Kodiak office steward, Philip Artamonovich Kashevarov, taught writing and mathematics. In 1822, Kashevarov was sent to St Petersburg to continue his education. By the end of his career, he had reached the rank of major general.

Soon after Father Gideon's departure, the monks separated: the monks Herman and Joseph remained to serve in Pavlovskaia Harbor, and Hieromonk Athanasius, in search of solitude, moved to Afognak Island, where there was an outpost of the company in which about twenty people lived.

"Often subject to bouts of depression, Hieromonk Athanasius moved along with his vestry to Afagnak Island, which neighbored Kodiak. Every year he visited Pavlovskaia Harbor during Great Lent for the services of Passion Week.[113] Due to poor health, the rest of the time he did not come to Kodiak."[114]

An understanding of Father Herman's life after 1807 is revealed in several letters to and from him, which are included below. By way of explanation, it should be noted that Alitak and Karluk are the names of Aleut villages on Kodiak Island; not far from Kodiak lies Malinovskaia, an outpost on an island of the same name. Ivan Ivanovich Banner was the manager of the Kodiak office of the company. Philip Kashevarov was the steward of that office; he ran the store. Ivan Kuglinov was Baranov's nephew and an English translator. Peter Kovrigin was a Kodiak Aleut and translator, who had worked for the company since 1790; he accompanied Billings' expedition of 1790–1792. Michael Bykadorov (Bykidorov) was one of Baranov's closest assistants. Athanasius Klimovskii was a Creole who later became an explorer of the Alaskan interior. He spent his last years on Spruce Island, where he died in 1868.

Your Honor! Most-Merciful Sire!

Father Herman!

I wish you many years of health. I want to inform you that I visited my father. I left here March 25, spent three nights on the road and after a snowstorm arrived in Alitak on the first day of Pascha. I stayed there for Bright Week, for the entire feast, and arrived here at the artel (Karluk) the eighth of this month. I do not know what is next. I spoke myself with my father about marriage.

He said, "If you want to, then why not get married; why should you live this way." Now, he says he would like to come here, to Karluk, in May for putting up bullheads[115] and boletus.[116] From here he wants to go to Malinova, to Afognak, and to you, in the Harbor. He wanted to take me there to get me married and now I do not know what to do. Will you and Ivan Ivanovich allow me be in the Harbor?

Lopatin claimed that Mr Bikodorov told you about all my indecent conduct, and that Kovrigin informed the Office in his report. You are aware that now my case depends only on your mercy. If indeed you are not pleased with all my indecent conduct, then have mercy and forgive me, a poor man, since you believe in our Savior, in Jesus Christ. For His sake, I implore you: it often happens that though a person is not guilty, yet that cannot be determined from the outside. If you can find mercy, forgive me, and then I will assume that His Honor, Alexander Andreevich (Baranov) has also forgiven me.

Relying on your mercy, I have dared to ask and to labor so that you do not deny me your mercy. If it is possible, my dear

Father Herman, please, ask Father Joseph if he got the goods from Philip Kashevarov from the previous order. I did not get some of it. Father Joseph himself knows which things I did not get, which could be used for a stamp. If you would be so kind, I have very little tobacco, not even one leaf. I didn't write to Ivan Ivanovich [Banner] about any of this; please either write a note or tell the man carrying this letter, Timothy, whether or not I should come to you with my father to the Harbor, with my bride; I will do as you instruct me. Besides this, Athanasius Klimovskii is coming to you to the Harbor; I do not know his plans.

The obedient servant and disciple of your Most-Merciful Sire

Paramon Chumovitskii

1809, April 27. Karluk

Address: My Most-Merciful Sire, Hieromonk Father Herman[117] of the Spiritual Mission, to his honor in the St Pavlovskaia Harbor[118]

Your Reverence, Most-Merciful Sire,

Father Herman!

I assure Your Reverence of my great esteem. And besides that, I ask that you generously forgive my offense of having been so bold as to dare to burden you with these, my simple lines. But I consider it my unavoidable duty to not miss this good opportunity to report to you, my benefactor. For I am disposed to you with an open and candid heart—disposed to your compassions and guidance, which I consider sufficient, for even to this day they remain fresh in my memory and have left a permanent impression.

Beyond that, I dare to inform you about myself. Now, thank God, I am healthy, by your holy prayers and the mercy of my dear uncle Alexander Andreevich [Baranov]. There is enough of everything, though I dare to burden you with my request—Your Reverence, would it not be possible to provide, if you have extra, various garden seeds, particularly garlic and onion. I suppose that you surely have some, but not too many; so if it is possible I most humbly ask you to supply them, since there is none here. Please also supply other seeds as well.

Out of gratitude for not forsaking me, I give Your Reverence my goodwill.

Your Reverence, Merciful Sire, I have the honor to always be your most-humble servant, Ivan Kuglinov

12 September, 1810

Novoarkhangel'sk[119] fortress and port[120]

In September 1807, the sloop *Neva* arrived in New Arkhangel'sk from Kronstadt, under the command of Ludwig (Leontii Adrianovich) von Hagemeister. The *Neva* arrived at Kodiak October 9, 1807; the vessel wintered there and then left for the Hawaiian Islands and Kamchatka. In the course of his many years of sailing the waters between Alaska, the Hawaiian Islands, and Kamchatka, Hagemeister wintered in Kodiak twice, in 1807–1808 and 1809–1810.

At those times, Father Herman made a great impression on Captain Hagemeister, who came from Baltic

German stock and was a Lutheran. Simeon Ianovskii, who later served under the command of Hagemeister, wrote,

> Several years ago, he [Father Herman] converted one sea captain H. from Lutheranism to Orthodoxy. This captain was well educated; in addition to many sciences, he knew languages— Russian, German, French, English, and some Spanish—yet despite all of this, he could not counter Father Herman's persuasiveness and proofs. He changed his faith and was united to the Orthodox Church by chrismation. When he was leaving America, the elder said to him in parting: "See that if the Lord takes your spouse from you, that you by no means marry a German; if you marry a German she will certainly entice you away from Orthodoxy."[121]

Hagemeister gave his word, but did not keep it. After the death of his first wife, he married a German again. He died suddenly, without repentance, in 1833 at the age of 53.

Father Herman mentioned his meetings with Hagemeister in two of his letters to Baranov. The first of these is from the fall of 1809. The "terrible occurrence" about which Father Herman writes was the conspiracy in the summer of 1809 of Russian *promyshlenniki* in New Archangel'sk to kill Baranov. The famine of the winter of 1808–1809 in New Archangel'sk and Baranov's cruel treatment of the *promyshlenniki* were the reason for this conspiracy. Mentioned in the letter are Arina Aleksandrovna, Baranov's daughter Irina, and Christopher

Prianishnikov, son of the former translator for the mission, Osip Prianishnikov.

Most-Merciful Sire,

Alexander Andreevich.

The Father of compassions and God Almighty, preserving the world, also preserves your life and well-being; to Him alone should be given glory and thanksgiving unto the ages.

Your terrible occurrence strongly compels one to contemplate the misfortunes and dangers which surround us, and from which Divine Providence protects us. Just as convincingly it compels us to admit our feebleness and powerlessness, and to seek Fatherly protection and the defense of the Almighty. The Wisdom and Word of God brought us to this state. He came down by the will of the Heavenly Father in the guise of our likeness in the flesh, woven by Divine power from the Most Pure Virgin, for the sake of our salvation. He was a man and deigned to teach . . . and by this He reminds us, from what kind of Father do we have our existence, so that we would seek our Heavenly Homeland and our eternal inheritance.

Along with this I consider it necessary to inform you of the following: I have received the first package with honey and the most recent one with nuts and wheat, as well as garlic and onion. I am grateful, but the copy[122] which was included with it, despite all my love for the orphans, obligates me beyond my strength . . . it is matter of virtue . . . I earnestly would like to serve, but the virtue of not having cares and a natural inclination to solitude—these are great obstacles. . . . Therefore, it is in no way possible to fulfill that obligation, although I would like to. . . .

Everything is peaceful and prosperous on Kodiak; all are well and healthy. In addition, Antipatr Aleksandovich is studying with the boys in your house, but not all [the students] are gathered yet.

The *Neva* did not forget to say goodbye to us, but . . . bad weather forced it to winter over with us, and on November 8 Leontii Andrianovich [Hagemeister], as a sign of his love for this region and indelible memories of this place, was kind enough to baptize Christopher's son, Dmitry, along with Arina Aleksandrovna; he was born October 26.

We baptized the Mednovskii *toion* Kiltys on your names-day. We named you the godfather and gave him your name. I congratulate you on your new son; I ask you to take care of him . . . and to give fatherly love and to be a benefactor of all the residents of that region.

There is no [ship] from Okhotsk yet . . . it is not known if they are wintering over at Unalaska. Despite one's innate curiosity, I truly hold in high regard the current quiet here. On a feast, when we gather, [we discuss] either our own quietude or comfort, or we recall some archival information, and time flies. . . .

In between we were often occupied by various opinions about your conditions. The rumors we had were very bad. We were greatly disturbed by doubts and tedium the whole summer, until we received reliable information. A variety of rumors reached us, so that we even expected some kind of attacks on us, but thanks be to God, the *Neva* provided us with information about you and then also about the Al'bion voyagers.[123] I regret our failure to settle that place. . . .

However, I wish joyous success for your good intentions; may they be the seeds of heavenly fruit; may the ascetic labors of patience be crowned in eternity with an immortal crown, which I, most-merciful Sire, wholeheartedly wish for you.

1809

I hope to not bother you, by mentioning a small request. Christopher's mother, who was married to a Lis'evsk [an Aleut], was living at Sitka. The man, it was learned, died, and if she has not married another man, then would it be possible to have the kindness to send her back to Kodiak to her son?[124]

The next letter of Father Herman to Baranov can be dated to the fall of 1810. The start of this letter tells about the conversations of Father Herman with Hagemeister, in which the elder convinced him to stay on Kodiak until April 10 and, if necessary, to head for California. This letter shows what enormous influence Father Herman could have on people. By April 1810, Hagemeister's term of service in the RAC had expired several months before and he had yet to return to St Petersburg through Siberia, which should have taken no less than six months; nonetheless, he was ready to stay in America under the influence of conversations with Father Herman.

Anna Grigorevna was Baranov's wife and Antipatr Aleksandrovich was his son, who at this time was thirteen years old. Ivan Kulikalov was the schoolteacher. Later, he was transferred to be the scribe in the settlement of Ross in California. Those arrested were five *promyshlenniki* who formed the conspiracy to kill Baranov. The conspiracy was uncovered, and the criminals were sent to Siberia for trial.

Here [on Kodiak] raising livestock and cutting hay happens almost all summer; due to the cold, they barely are able to cut and carry wood the whole winter.

Due to dampness and the climate the building itself is neither solid nor good. The long winter, in this, as in other things, ties your hands and makes everything difficult. Everywhere you go the chance is never missed to go into the most detailed explanations of the ships themselves, which stand idle the whole winter in the cold of the north. There is also discussion of the expanse of the mainland, the forests, hunting, and countless advantages to the south. This is how it was possible to influence Leontii Andrianovich [Hagemeister], so that he readily agreed to wait for you [Baranov] until April 10, when before he had decided to go to Kamchatka in the middle of March.

But he changed his plans, deciding to wait for you and, if you so desired, to take his vessel to go help our settlements. Similarly, I tried to explain to the *promyshlenniki* the inexpediency of the escape that occurred in California, by comparing it to the great profit for those who settle in those places and who will be faithful to our fatherland. Many of them, particularly those who are married, categorically assured me of their stead-fastness and cited their families as proof, saying it would be impossible to abandon them. And so we anxiously waited, but since it didn't happen, such is the will of the Lord.

We are now sending you Anna Grigor'evna with all the children [to Sitka]. May God grant that they successfully travel to you and that you joyfully see each other. I advised her to winter with us and to travel in the spring for safety's sake, but she and Antipatr Aleksandrovich did not agree out of fear for the severe winter weather and cold, which I thoroughly regret. I have great praise for Anna Grigor'evna; based on many of her deeds, she seems to me to not be foolish in the least. In particular, before the departure—and no one had instructed her—she asked that liturgy and a moleben be served, so as to confess along with all her servants and to commune of the Holy Mysteries. We wholly marveled at this sensible action.

I cannot tell you anything about Antipatr Aleksandrovich; I know little about how he lived with us. Before sending this [letter], I was at a reception, where I heard it said that he and my Joseph had downed a lot of vodka, but it seemed to me that that was said primarily out of jealousy, for some reason. I did not know how to satisfy them. I was afraid of some kind of wrath, since there is a fair amount of hatred of me due to your favor toward me, but let God take care of them. I seek nothing; they are free to do as they want, but I will rely on God.

We have no school in the Harbor [in the village of Pav-lovskaia Harbor]. Ivan Kulikalov was moved to the office; I was not told a word. Last year he asked me, but I didn't dare allow it without asking you. So now I ask you not to be angry with me—the decision was not mine. A portion of the young schoolchildren in Karluk are under Chumovitskii's supervision. Only Christopher [Prianishnikov] remains at the church and lives with us. To my amazement, despite such a state of freedom, the jealousy does not die down. I implore you to not abandon this orphan.

Concerning Zosima Fedorovich Bazhenov, he mentioned one of your orders that I do not know. He rendered us considerable good deeds and attentiveness; although he is now no longer in the Harbor, I am very grateful to you.

At the start of your letter you made mention of a suggestion of mine about the prisoners. I consulted my draft of the letter, but it is not mentioned there. I remember nothing of what was in the final version written to you; excuse me.

As for myself, I will be so bold as to inform you that after this interruption I remain, by the mercy of God, alive, healthy, and safe—and hoping for some more new information from you, if you will be so kind as to satisfy my curiosity. I ask you to not be angry with us, but we cannot serve you this way; we spent a year as if in isolation, not hearing anything from anywhere.

There is nothing to write about Kodiak; everyone is alive and well. As to how they live, I think, they write enough that there is nothing for me to add. It is inappropriate for me to interfere in the affairs of others. I get along with everyone though some curse me; I cannot shed that.

Forgive me; forgive me, kind Sire; forgive me.

With all my heart I wish you true prosperity.

The most zealous servant of Your Great Honor, my Sire,

(Postscript)

I do not intend to suggest this out of daring and impudence, but I fear upsetting you with my silence about our needs.

During your stay on Kodiak you saw fit to order that the company return those provisions that had been taken from us (in 1805) by Nicholas Peterovich [Rezanov]. After your departure, Ivan Ivanovich [Banner] refused, despite our assurance of that. He claimed that without you he could not dare to do this.

After the arrival of the *Neva* last winter, he was afraid that we would ask him [for rations] for the sailors. He himself ordered that we receive provisions, but soon thereafter he took them back, leaving us a portion. Recently, he grudgingly gave Joseph and me a three-pood [108-pound] container with just two poods [72 pounds] of rusk. I hear that you have a considerable amount of rusk and provisions in Sitka; would you be so generous as to authorize for transport from Sitka to us whatever quantity God gives you to understand is a year's supply of provisions: rusk and grain, along with wine for church. We very rarely serve liturgy due to a shortage of wine, but soon we will not have anything at all with which to serve.

Wretched Herman.[125]

In time, life on Kodiak returned to normal and flowed along its typical course. With each year, Father Herman was more and more burdened by the secular society that surrounded him. In the end, he decided to seclude him-self. He turned the direction of the church over to monk Joseph and moved to the uninhabited Spruce Island, which was a two-hour *baidarka* ride from the village of Pavlovskaia Harbor.

CHAPTER 3

On Spruce Island: A Saint in the Wilderness

There is no precise information as to when Father Herman moved to Spruce Island. It is only possible to say that it happened in the period between 1811 and 1817. Everything there reminded him of the Valaam Monastery, which is located on an island in Lake Ladoga—the island set in water, the coniferous forest, and the enormous piles of boulders on the shore. Father Herman called his new residence "New Valaam."

Spruce Island is not very large, around forty-six miles in diameter. It is separated from Kodiak Island on one side by Ouzinkie Strait, which is 1.3 miles wide. It was almost seven miles from Father Herman's cell to the village of Pavlovskaia Harbor. All of Spruce Island was covered in a tall forest. A spring flowed near Father Herman's residence, which among locals was renowned as miracle working; there have been instances of healings from its waters.

At the start of his stay on Spruce Island, Father Herman excavated a dugout, which was his cell throughout the summer. By winter he had built a small log cell, in which he resided until the end of his days. A small bench, covered with an old deer hide with fur faded from age, served as Father Herman's bed. He used two bricks as a pillow. These lay at the head of the bed under the hide, so that strangers could not see them. There was no blanket; instead, he used a wooden board, which sat on the stove during the day. Father Herman called this board his blanket and willed that his mortal remains be covered by it. It was the exact height of Father Herman. In time, a small chapel and house for guests were built not far from his cell. The guesthouse also accommodated a school for orphans, students of Father Herman.

By the time of his move to Spruce Island, Father Herman possessed many spiritual gifts. With the vigilant eyes of the soul, he saw angels of God and dark spirits of evil. Initially, Father Herman lived on Spruce Island entirely alone. When they asked him, "Father Herman, how do you live alone in the woods? Don't you become bored?" He replied, "No! I am not alone there! God is there, just as God is everywhere! Holy angels are there! And how is it possible to become bored with them? With whom is it more pleasant to converse, with people or with angels? With angels, of course!"[126]

Father Herman left his island extremely rarely. According to Father Joseph, if Father Herman had to spend the night elsewhere, then he only stayed in his old cell in Pavlovskaia Harbor and didn't lay down to sleep at all, so that the bed made up for him was found completely untouched. Likewise, when he was at home on Spruce Island, if he spent the night in a soul-saving conversation with one of his guests, then he wouldn't go to sleep.

Father Herman's clothes were one and the same both winter and summer. On his bare skin he wore a fur parka; over it, a cassock and riasa. He wore a klobuk on his head and boots on his feet. This is how he dressed in all weather: in great heat, in rain, and in the hardest frost. He ate very little: some fish and vegetables. His body, worn out by labors, vigils, and fasting, was humbled by wearing chains weighing thirteen and a half pounds.

When not in services, the elder spent all his time laboring. A garden, in which he prepared beds and planted barley, potatoes, cabbage, and other vegetables, was set up not far from his cell. He laid up mushrooms and fish for winter. The woven basket in which Father Herman carried seaweed from the shore to fertilize the soil was so large that the average man could lift it only with great difficulty, but the elder, to the surprise of all, carried it for great distances without assistance. It was once observed how Father Herman carried a log that four men could lift only with difficulty. This is how the elder labored. Everything that he acquired with such hard labor he gave to the poor and orphans. He particularly loved children; he treated them with rusks and baked pretzels for them. The little ones responded to him with love.

But this was the external side of the life of the elder. "His primary occupation," as His Grace Peter, bishop of New Arkhangel'sk wrote in the 1860s, "was exercise in spiritual ascetic struggles in his secluded cell, where no one saw him. Outside the cell it was only heard that he sang and served services according to the monastic rule."[127]

The priest S. Liashevskii saw in the external side of St Herman's life an expression of the Christian ascetic struggle of being a fool-for-Christ. He wrote,

> Wishing to hide the difficulty of his ascetic struggles from those around him, as he hid his 13.5-lb chains and brick pillow . . . St Herman could not hide his "blanket" from those around him, which he named in such a humorous form, which is an indication of a fool-for-Christ. Wishing to hide their ascetic struggles, they turned everything into a joke, they behaved like "fools" for Christ. We see that St Herman had all the super-human ascetic struggles which are characteristic of fools-for-Christ, such as walking barefoot in the winter, wearing summer clothes in the winter, and so on. The only difference is that St Herman tried to hide them carefully: his disciple Gerasim only accidentally saw him walking barefoot in the winter and carrying an enormously heavy log.[128]

The Kodiak Aleut Ignatius Alig-iaga said of the life of the elder, "*Appa*[129] led a difficult life, and no one can imitate his life!"

In July 1818, a visit to Kodiak Island was made by the crew of the naval sloop *Kamchatka,* under the command of the Captain Second-Class Basil Michaelovich Golovnin. Under government orders, he was assigned to be the inspector of the Russian colony in America. Having arrived on Kodiak, Golovnin began to hear a multitude of complaints.

Golovnin wrote, "Meanwhile, both Russian and native residents petition me daily, all of whom were bringing complaints about their rulers. Some of these complaints, surely, were justified, but others were empty and unfounded. In order to better ascertain the real condition of affairs here, I addressed by letter the head of the religious mission here, monk Herman—an intelligent and pious man, it is said, and one whom the greater part of the residents here cannot praise sufficiently. He sent me much very important information and confirmed it by his own hand."[130]

Relying on notes from sailors who had visited Kodiak previously, Golovnin asked Father Herman three questions. First, was the number of local residents shrinking as a result of young men being sent hunting for several years by the company, leaving their wives and children to live in poverty and starve without breadwinners? If Father Herman confirmed this was the case, could he supply Golovnin with the parish registers to find out the number of births and deaths during the time of the existence of the mission on Kodiak from 1794 to 1818?

Golovnin wrote regarding the reply to this question,

> On these matters the head of the mission, monk Herman, informed me:
>
> . . . that the Company never gave them the means to keep parish registers. Neither did they inform them of births or of deaths and that the Aleuts often died in great number at distant outposts; therefore the mission has no registers.

Second, were the Russian *promyshlenniki* taking the wives and daughters of Kodiak Aleuts to live with them in depravity? Concerning this second question, Golovnin wrote,

> Why did I demand information from the missionary Herman as to if such accusations are justified? Since faith and fear of God are the principal and primary foundation of all well-organized societies, without which there can be neither order nor justice, and since they are all the more necessary in such remoteness, where the company is served by people not of the best conduct, then I also wanted to learn from the missionary mentioned if the company takes any measures to support the faith and piety among its employees, and their loyalty to the Sovereign. For example: On every holy day is a service held in church and are people off work on such days; does the company require them to keep the fast and partake of Holy

Communion at the appropriate time according ecclesiastical rules and regulations; does it bring newly baptized Aleuts for the oath of allegiance; and so on.

Father Herman's reply to this second question was that because of the unrestricted power of the local authorities it was true that the female sex endures offenses and dishonor, and that no measures of any kind are taken for the support of the faith and morality.

Third, how were punishments and trials conducted on Kodiak? Father Herman responded that that an institution akin to a court or an investigative commission has never existed in the Company colonies and that all matters are decided and punishment is carried out by the will of one man.[131]

Among others, Grigorii Pavlov, an Aleut from the Aleutian Islands, and Alexander Golovnin and Fedor Balokhov, Russian settlers, appealed to Captain Golovnin with complaints. The Aleut said that he had been hired to work for Shelikhov for three years in 1794 and that it was now 1818, but they had not yet released him. Alexander Golovnin and Balokhov explained that of the thirty-five settlers who were there in 1794, only a few remained alive.

"The head of the mission, Herman, confirmed in absolutely everything the substance and truth of the complaint both of these settlers and of the aforementioned Aleut Pavlov."[132]

"In the meanwhile, as long as I was occupied with these inquiries," continued Golovnin, both natives and company *promyshlenniki* came to me every day with complaints. And although they were all questioned separately and on different days, they said one and the same thing. The essence of all the general complaints of the natives, selected from the elders and *toions* of five different villages . . . consists of the following:

1. Company managers force the residents to work at all times and in bad weather, as a result of which many of them fall ill and have their health permanently undermined or die an early death.

2. They send them on hunts to distant places and often for many years, where they are subject to danger from the aggressive native peoples and are often killed by them. Additionally, their families, due to a lack of young and healthy people, are deprived of the means to find food for themselves, since in the summer they have to both work for the company and lay up stores for themselves for the winter.

3. The residents who remain on Kodiak are for the most part elderly or cripples and women, but even they are continually occupied with work for the benefit of the company. They lay up and cure stores of fish for the entire winter not only for the *promyshlenniki*, but also for the company pigs. They also gather berries in the fall. As a result, they often are forced to eat tree bark and shells, or dead animals that happen to be tossed up onto the beach.

4. The company forces the residents to catch wild cats, and to kill sea lions and other marine animals. From the skins of

the former and the insides of the latter, their wives and daughters sew dresses and shoes by the order of the company stewards. The company pays the residents for beavers with these very same dresses and shoes. The goods that the company brings are sold at exorbitant, intolerable prices. . . .

5. Finally they complained that they are often subject to undeserved severe beatings and offenses from the company stewards. Due to the extreme deficiencies, difficult labor, and dangerous hunts, from the beatings and continual lengthy times that young people are apart from their wives, from year to year their population noticeably declines. And they think, that if they will continue to treat them the way that they currently do, they will completely disappear. The fewer of them there are, the more difficult the work is for those who remain. In the end they will have to flee into the mountains and live on roots alone.[133]

Concerning the general condition of the spiritual mission, Golovnin wrote,

From 1794 to 1818, that is for 24 years, the Company not only did not give the spiritual mission Bibles, the New Testament, or other religious books, but also did not even provide basic readers to teach reading to the children, nor even wax candles and wine to celebrate liturgy. From the laborers of thirty-five families, now [1818] there remains only three men and one woman. . . . And so Shelikhov has shown the world, that there is no difference between big and small merchants.

As the shop keeper in an arcade swears and makes oaths by the Lord's name in order to sell his goods for a few pennies more than their actual price, so did Shelikhov use the name of Christ and His holy faith in order to deceive the government and to lure thirty-five unfortunate families to the wild land of America, where they perished for his profit and for that of his cohorts.[134]

Then Father Herman had a conversation with the crew of the sloop *Kamchatka*. Here is how Simeon Ivanovich Ianovskii recalled this:

Once they invited the elder to the frigate which had come from St Petersburg. The captain of the frigate was a consummate scholar, highly educated, and sent to America by Imperial orders in order to inspect all the colonies. With him there were about twenty-five officers, who were also educated people.

In such company sat a smallish hermit in tattered clothes. With the wisdom of his conversation he brought all of his educated companions to such a state that they didn't know how to answer him. The captain himself said, "We were speechless, like fools before him."

Father Herman gave them all one common question, "What do you, gentlemen, love most of all and what would each of you desire for his own happiness?"

Various answers sprang up: one wanted riches; another wanted a position of rank; one, a beautiful wife; or an excellent vessel on which he would be in command; and so on in a similar vein.

"Is it not true," said Father Herman in response to them, "that all your various desires can be summed up in one—that each of you wishes that, which in his understanding, he considers to be the very best and worthy of love?"

"Yes, that's it!" everyone replied.

"What do you say then," he continued, "Can there be anything better, above everything, more exalted and by nature more worthy of love than our very Lord Himself, Jesus Christ, Who created us, adorned us with such perfections, gave life to everyone, keeps us all, feeds us, loves everyone, and Who is love Himself, more excellent than all people? Must we not, therefore, love God above all and desire and seek Him most of all?"

Everyone began to reply, "Well, yes! This goes without saying! This is self evident!"

"And do you love God?" asked the elder then.

Everyone answered, "Of course, we love God. How could you not love God?"

"But I, a sinner, have been trying for more than forty years to love God and cannot say that I love Him completely," objected Father Herman, and he began to show how God should be loved.

"If we love someone," he said, "we always remember him; we try to please him; day and night our heart is occupied with that object. Is this the very way, gentlemen, that you love God? Do you turn to Him often; do you keep Him in remembrance

always; do you pray to Him and keep His holy commandments always?" They had to admit that they did not.

"For our own good, for our happiness," concluded the elder,
"let us at least give ourselves a promise that from this day, from
this hour, from this minute, we will now try to love God most
of all and to fulfill His holy will!"[135]

This is the kind of exceptional, wise conversation
that Father Herman held in the company of the privi-
leged class of that time. Among the officers of the sloop
Kamchatka who were present during this discussion were
future key leaders of Russian America: M. I. Murave'ev,
F. P. Wrangell, and A. K. Etolin. There were also future
famous seafarers such as F. P. Litke, F. F. Matiushkin,
F. S. Lutkovskii, and P. T. Koz'min. Without a doubt, this
conversation was imprinted on the hearts of the listeners
for their whole life.

As a result of Golovnin's inspection trip, the main
office of the RAC in St Petersburg allowed the return to
Russia of the settlers I. M. Shchukin with his wife and
daughter, S. Krylatskii, F. Balakhov, and A. Golovin,
although they were sent to their homeland only in 1823.[136]

A letter of Father Herman to Baranov also pertains
to the middle or start of 1818. In January 1818, Baranov
was dismissed from his position as chief ruler of the Russian colonies in America and sent to Russia for trial and
harsh punishments. In his place, Captain Hagemeister
was appointed.

Sire!

I heard that the Lord God blessed you with material prosperity, and even abundance. And under our care, as you yourself know, is the church property, consisting not only of things belonging to the church, but all household things as well.

All of this does not belong to us, but is God's property, cared for by us only for the poor. Due to this, I must remind you about things taken by you from us for the shortest of time: table settings, tablecloths, napkins, knives, and forks.

Perhaps, such a long time has not allowed forgetfulness to cloud your memory, then in order that we, for our carelessness, and you, though perhaps due to forgetfulness, not be given over to the wrath of God for the lack of care for that which belongs to the poor—to escape such danger would you not deign to return them; if not the same ones, then others of comparable worth.

Your humble servant, of my kind Sire.[137]

Kyrill Timofeyevich Khlebnikov, steward of the RAC, arrived in Alaska along with Hagemeister and was assigned director of the main office of the company in New Archangel'sk (Sitka). Not being personally acquainted with Father Herman, he sent the elder a book of religious content. In his reply letter, Father Herman wrote,

Kind Sire, Kyrill,

I do not know your patronymic; forgive me.

I received the book you sent. I offer you my gratitude. This kindness you have shown me, a wretch, is all the more appreciated since throughout all my days here I have mostly experienced disdain, reproach, and mockery from my own Russians. I have already become accustomed to this, and by habit, I believe that my lowliness, in fact, deserves this.

And yet you, having neither seen nor knowing me at all, have bestowed such kindness on me—I am greatly astonished and thank you, kind Sire.

Your humble servant

The wretched Herman.

There is much I would like to say about the book, yet the weakness of my eyes has not allowed even a little, since I already write with great difficulty; additionally they say that the ship will depart soon.

December 28, 1818[138]

Not seeking anything for himself in this life, Father Herman did not fear the strong of this world. With meek love, regardless of the person, he denounced many of an intemperate life, unworthy behavior, and oppression of the Kodiak Aleuts. Therefore, there were people who slandered the elder; moreover they did this so skillfully that even well-intentioned people could not notice the lies beneath the veneer of truth. It can be said that the Lord alone preserved the elder.

Hagemeister lasted as the main ruler of the Russian colonies in America for only a few months. In October 1818, the young officer Simeon Ivanovich Ianovskii became the main ruler. Without even knowing the elder, and only as a result of nothing but denunciations against him (surely from Baranov, whose son-in-law he was), Ianovskii wrote to St Petersburg about the necessity of removing Father Herman from America. He explained this by claiming that the elder incited the Kodiak Aleuts to demonstrate against the Russian authorities.

Having learned of the appointment of a new ruler, Father Herman wrote Ianovskii a letter at once, in which he wrote about Alaska and its residents:

> The Creator was pleased to give our beloved homeland this region, which is like a newborn infant, since as yet it has neither strength for any sort of knowledge, nor sense; it demands not only protection, but even support, due to its weakness and feebleness—the result of its infancy. It has as yet no ability to make its own request about these very matters, but since this people's state of prosperity has been bestowed for an unknown period of time by Divine Providence into the hands of the resident Russian authorities, which now have been entrusted to your control, for this reason:
>
> I, the most-humble servant of these local peoples and their caretaker, write with tears of blood, in the name of those placed before you, my request to you. Be a father and protector to us; we, of course, do not possess eloquence, but with the mute voice of an infant we say, "Wipe away the tears of our defenseless orphans; assuage the sorrows of a languishing heart; let us understand what joy means!"

In this short sentence, most-kind Sire, by your subtlety of mind and focused attention you can find the breadth and extent of this people's tribulations. We abide in hope of what favorable disposition to the fate of the poor the Creator will pour out on your heart.[139]

Father Herman always helped his spiritual children in whatever way he could: he asked for mercy from the authorities to those who had committed offenses; he interceded on behalf of those accused; he helped the poor and orphans—and people often called on him at Spruce Island. Some sought advice; others complained of oppression; and still more entreated assistance—every one received satisfaction from the elder, to which the following letter attests.

Your Reverence, kind Sire,
Batiushka![140] Father Herman.
I have dared to run to the feet of your Reverence to ask you, knowing your love for your fellowman, that you not deny your charitable goodwill to those who ask you for mercy.
For this sake even I, a sinner, was able to grasp for whose footsteps I could and to flatter myself with hope that you, *batiushka,* are not unaware that the time has now come to plant garden vegetables for our winter provisions. That is why I started a small garden plot and dug it up. As many seed potato pieces as I had in stock I planted, but there are not enough of them; if I had another half of a basket, I would be at ease. I

tell you in truth, *batiushka,* I have ground which remains dug and completely prepared, but I stopped after that and though I asked here and sought after them [the seed potato pieces], it was all to no avail, since everyone has their own garden. . . .

But now I find that I have no other recourse—what other option is there—I leave [my garden] to the will of God.

Such is my state while I make my appeal to your mercy. If you can help, *batiushka,* don't abandon me, for God's sake! Please grant me at least half a basket, with which you will do me, a sinful servant of God, an enormous favor, and by which you will ease my poverty when the Lord God Most-High ordains His land to prosper.

Also, if you have some turnip seeds, perhaps you could spare half a spoonful. I wanted enormously to come visit you myself, *batiushka*, but time didn't allow it. And so, in closing, I ask, *batiushka*, for your holy prayers and that you not forget us sinners in the future.

Your most-humble and most-loyal servant, Peter Mal'tsov.
May 23, 1819, from Pavlovskaia Harbor[141]

The letter from Father Herman, along with a personal meeting, completely changed Ianovskii's opinion of the elder. In the fall of 1819, Ianovskii completed a tour of all the Russian colonies in America. In November, he arrived in Kodiak, where he stayed for more than a month. In advance, even from Sitka, Ianovskii informed the venerable Herman that he would like to meet with him. Father Herman immediately appeared before Ianovskii and so captivated the young officer with his conversation that they began to meet weekly for spiritual conversations. Father Herman usually arrived by 7:00 p.m., and they conversed until midnight and sometimes even after midnight.

Ianovskii wrote,

I was thirty years old when I met Father Herman. It should be mentioned that I was trained at a naval college. I knew much science and had read widely, but, unfortunately, the science of sciences—that is, the Law of God—I hardly understood even superficially and what I did know was theoretical, not applied to life. I was a Christian only in name, while in my soul and my action, I was a free-thinker and a deist. In this I was like almost everyone who has been trained in colleges and official institutions. . . .

What is more, I did not acknowledge the divine nature and sanctity of our religion; I had read many of the godless essays of Voltaire and other philosophers of the eighteenth century.

Father Herman immediately noticed this and wanted to convert me. It was not easy! I had to be convinced, to be shown the holiness of our faith; this is why it required time, knowledge, and the ability to speak well and convincingly.

To my great surprise, this simple, uneducated monk, Father Herman, inspired by grace, spoke so forcefully, so wisely, and argued so convincingly that, it seemed to me, no erudition or earthly wisdom could hold out against his words! Father Herman truly had a great mind, sound thought, and had read many spiritual books; most importantly, he had the grace of God!

We spoke unceasingly: about love, about God, about eternity, about the salvation of the soul, about the Christian life, and other things. An unceasing flood of sweet conversation flowed from his mouth!

Through such constant talks and by the prayers of the holy elder, the Lord converted me wholly to the path of truth, and I became a true Christian. For all of this, I am obliged to Father Herman; he is my true benefactor.[142]

Although Father Herman, as a monk, was continually burdened by civil society and wished to distance himself from people, he had to carry the cross of a missionary to the end of his days. Ianovskii wrote, "It was his desire to retreat from the world, but seeing the deficiencies of his fellow brothers, he give spiritually beneficial advice to the people, in order to convert them to piety; he only does this due to the lack of confessors."[143]

Ianovskii once read Gabriel Romanovich Derzhavin's ode "God" to the elder.

> O Thou, who art infinite in space,
> Alive in the movement of matter,
> Pre-eternal in the flow of time,
> Without a face, yet a Deity in three persons!
> Whose spirit art everywhere present and indivisible,
> Who hath neither space nor cause,
> Whom no one can comprehend,

Whose Being fillest all things,

And containeth, createth, and preserveth them,

Thou, Whom we call: God. . . .

Father Herman asked, "Is it possible that a simple scholar wrote this?"

"Yes, a scholar, a poet," Ianovskii answered.

"This was written by divine inspiration," said the elder.

During one of their meetings, Ianovskii told the elder about events that had taken place in Spanish California.

In 1815, a hunting party of Kodiak Aleuts under the leadership of Boris Tarasov had been hunting sea animals along the shore of California. The wind blew their *baidarkas* to the shore. At the cape of San Pedro, Spanish soldiers captured them and took them to the mission in San Pedro. During this, the Spanish "mutilated many with their unsheathed sabers. They cut off the head of one of the Kodiak Islanders by the name of Chukagnak (Peter in baptism), and, meanwhile, stole their personal property and all the goods of the company."

Ianovskii himself wrote about this in detail:

Once I told him how the Spanish in California captured fourteen of our Aleuts and how the Jesuits tortured one Aleut, forcing all of them to accept the Catholic faith, to which the Aleuts would by no means agree, answering, "We are Christians; we are baptized," and showed them the crosses around their necks.

But the Jesuits objected: "No, you are heretics. If you do not agree to accept the Catholic faith, then we will torture you." They left them by twos in the dungeon until the evening to think it over. In the evening they came with lanterns and lit candles and began yet again to try to convince them to accept the Catholic faith. But the Aleuts, imbued with grace, firmly and decisively answered, "We are Christians, we will not change our faith."

Then these fanatics began to torture them—first one, while the other witnessed. First they cut off one joint from the toes, then the second joint—he endured everything, but only said, "I am a Christian and will not betray my faith." Next they cut off one joint from each finger, followed by the second joint; after that they cut off his feet and then his hands—his blood poured forth, but the martyr endured to the end. Without change he repeated this one phrase with such faith; he died from loss of blood.

They intended to torture others the next day, but on that very night an order was received from Monterey that all Russian Aleuts taken prisoner be sent without delay under escort to Monterey. Therefore in the morning, all of them, expect for the one who had died, were sent away. This was told to me by an Aleut eyewitness, a companion of the one tortured, who subsequently escaped from captivity. I reported this to the Central Administration in St Petersburg.

When I finished my story, Father Herman asked, "What was the name of this tortured Aleut?"

I answered, "Peter, but I can't remember his last name."

Then he stood in front of an icon, reverently crossed himself and said these words: "Holy New-Martyr Peter, pray to God for us."[144]

The historian A. A. Istomin described this event as follows:

In the mission of San Pedro the Kodiaks were offered to accept Catholicism, but they refused. After a little while, Tarasov and the majority of the Kodiaks were transferred to Santa Barbara, but I. Kyglaia and the wounded Chukagnak from the village Kaguiak were left in San Pedro. They were kept there for several days without water and food with Indian convicts. Once at night, they were again ordered to accept Catholicism, "which under such extreme conditions they resolved not to do." At dawn a Catholic priest came to the prison with several Indians. The Kodiaks were called out of the prison. The Indians surrounded them, and the priest ordered to cut off Chukagnak's fingers at the joints on both hands and to cut off his hands. Then they disemboweled the dying Kodiak. When they gave the missionary some sort of paper, the execution was stopped. After he read it, he ordered them to bury Chukagnak's body in the ground.[145]

A Kodiak Aleut named Ivan Keeplii (some sources call him Kykhliai) witnessed Peter Chukagnak's martyric death. He was able to escape from captivity to the Spanish. He was picked up by the RAC's Russian vessel

Il'mena and taken to Fort Ross, from where he returned to New Arkhangel'sk in 1819.[146]

In the fall of 1819, a flu epidemic was brought to New Arkhangel'sk and then to Kodiak by the crew of an American vessel, which had arrived from Java. Most likely, it was the crew of the *Eagle* under the command of Thomas Mick. In Pavlovskaia Harbor, fifty-one people died from the flu. The epidemic quickly spread throughout Aleut settlements. The mortality rate was so high that entire Aleut families died. The bodies of the deceased stayed in houses for many days because there was no one to bury them.

Ianovskii wrote,

> During my stay on Kodiak Island an infectious, deadly, mass epidemic, or plague, which began with a fever, heavy congestion, and shortness of breath and ended with convulsions; after three days a person died!
>
> There was no doctor and no medicine there. The disease quickly spread throughout the settlement [Pavlovskaia Harbor] and soon crossed over to all the nearby settlements. Father Herman tirelessly visited the sick with great self-sacrifice. Not sparing himself, as a cleric he encouraged them to endure, to pray, and to repent, and he prepared them for death. . . . The illness affected everyone, even children who were being breastfed. In my family, my wife and child, who was being breast-fed, were both ill, as was I. The mortality rate was so high that for three days there were not enough people to dig

graves; the bodies piled up without being buried! Fortunately, it was below freezing, so that there was no smell.

I cannot imagine anything more dismal and more horrifying than that sight which struck me when I visited an Aleutian *kazhim*. This is a large barn, or barracks with bunks, in which the Aleuts live with their families. Up to 100 people could be housed in it. I went around to everyone: chatting, asking, advising, encouraging, comforting. Some were already dead, becoming cold whilst still next to the living; others were dying—groaning, crying—it rends the heart!

I saw already-dead mothers across whose cooling breasts a hungry infant crawled, crying out and searching for food—in vain! My heart bled from pity, seeing the staggering horror of this sad picture of death. It seems that if someone could paint the total horror of it with a worthy brush, then it would arouse the fear of death even in a hardened heart.[147]

During this epidemic, which lasted for more than a month, only Father Herman tirelessly visited the sick. Those Kodiak Aleuts who remained among the living, of course, loved Father Herman even more, because by risking his life, he had shown his love for them during the terrible calamity that had beset them.

Among those who died was the wife of Christopher Osipovich Prianishnikov, the church chanter; he was left with five children after her death. Prianishnikov was still officially listed as a teacher in the school, but in 1821 he was relieved of his duties "due to poor health and inattention to the services."

The Lord sent Father Herman another trial during the epidemic. As a hermit monk who continually sought out isolation, he had to take upon himself the upbringing of a two-year-old orphan, Gerasim Ivanovich Zyrianov. It can be said that for all practical purposes Father Herman adopted the child, since the boy was in danger of dying and Father Herman was the only person who could save him. Throughout the rest of his life, Father Herman fulfilled without complaint his new parental role as an extension of his missionary duty, an additional service to which the Lord had called him.

In December 1819, Father Herman delivered this parting message to Ianovskii, who was married to Baranov's daughter, Irina: "You are heading to Russia, to Petersburg—don't take your wife there. She was born here and has not seen the wide world, neither its captivating luxuries nor its temptations and vices. It would be better to leave her at your mother's, in Carpatho-Russia, while you travel on business to Petersburg."[148]

Ianovskii gave his word, but did not keep it. The Ianovskiis arrived in St Petersburg at the start of 1822, where the maelstrom of the high life surrounded them. Time passed unnoticeably, but after a few months Irina became tired of society life, of the endless round of balls, receptions, and dinner parties. It was then that Ianovskii remembered the warning of Father Herman. He took his wife to his mother in the country, but it was too late. Irina melted down, like a candle, from an unknown illness and died quietly in the start of 1824 at the age of twenty.

Ianovskii later bitterly regretted his disobedience. He wrote,

> My love, did you have a feeling that you were leaving your homeland forever . . . Many Creoles (more than twelve) had been taken from there to St Petersburg for studies in various fields, particularly navigation and shipbuilding. They were well cared for; they were deprived of nothing. Yet only two of them returned; the rest all died of melancholy and got consumption from the climate.
>
> That was the lot that awaited you, my priceless and beloved soul mate. . . . How could I have understood that the Russian capital would be your grave in the prime of your life! If I had known that, then I would have never, ever brought you to Russia. I would not have made you part with your homeland; it would have been better for me to stay in the desolate wilderness of America.[149]

Later, recalling his talks with the elder, Ianovskii said, "The meaning of Christian love is not the same as worldly love! What did he expect from me? What was he looking for? He only wished to save a lost sheep!" After the death of Irina, he married a second time in 1826. From this marriage, he had four children. In 1864, he went to a monastery in Kaluga. He accepted the monastic schema. He reposed January 6, 1876.

At the end of 1819, the correspondence of the monks of Valaam Monastery with Father Herman was renewed when he received a letter from Hegumen Jonathan. In response, he wrote,

Your Reverence, kind Sire, *Batiushka*, Father Jonathan with all the kind and most considerate Brothers in Christ, I wish that you rejoice in the Lord.

To our great surprise, your much desired and very kind, though unexpected letter, the appearance of which was even contrary to all expectations, illumined us—dismally remote by a great distance and much time—with the light of gladness, like joyous lightning on a dark night covered by the deep darkness of oblivion. The letter which you sent on November 8, 1818, arrived to us on November 10, 1819.

We find no means nor ways in which to thank you for your love, besides this insignificant, wretched scribbling of ours, in which at the outset we now offer our wholehearted thanks. And we ask, if it will be possible for your part, to favor us, as you already have, with your presence by letter. And to inform us, how Father Nazarius left Valaam Monastery for Sarov Monastery. Was it by some necessity, or by his own desire? In which year and month did he die? Also, how many hieromonks and hierodeacons are there in your holy Valaam Monastery? Who are they; are there any of our former acquaintances or are they all new?

We ask you, since you deigned to remember us and visit us through your letter, to remember us and to commemorate our wretchedness before God Almighty in your holy prayers.

We are not overwhelmed by ocean waves, but in this deceptive and highly troubled world "we are buffeted, and have no certain dwelling place,"[150] according to the Apostle's word, although we do not have that Grace, which the Holy Apostles had. But our battle is with the same incorporeal "principalities, against powers, against the rulers of darkness of this world, against spiritual wickedness in high places"[151] who try to catch all travelers bound for our heavenly home-land, and to hold them and to not release them. According to the words of the St Peter, "your adversary the devil, as a roar-ing lion, walketh about, seeking whom he may devour"[152] in which case we, weak and feeble, of course, have need to seek help from your holy prayers. Do not forget, our most kind Fathers, do not forget to remember our poverty before the Almighty Heavenly King; this we ask of all in your holy community.

We have the honor to inform you of our country and land and our condition. Our country of America is known to you. The main island is Kodiak, on which there is a company port and the Holy Resurrection Church. There is a house there that was given to us by the company at the time we arrived here. The country is cold, though the winters are not that cold. They are variable, snow and rain alternately. Summer does not begin early and is cool. Of garden vegetables, only turnips, radishes, and potatoes grow, but nothing else. The local vegetables are tubers. The first is called *sarana*, which is a little bitter, but very popular. It is first boiled and then mixed with berries, called *shiksha,* and then add whale blubber. This is a fairly good, staple dish for us. The other is called *makarsha*. It is small and hard to gather; it uses both raw and boiled. The taste is a little nutty, but there is just not enough of it. In terms of berries, the raspberries are not Russian, but of another variety; there are also cowberries and cloudberries, but in small quantities. Bilberries are in good supply, but most of all we collect a decent quantity of *shiksha*; in the winter is it prepared with whale blubber, and sometime with *sarana*. We have it on Valaam, though it is not used, but called *voronitsa*. We have an enormous quantity of fish in a multitude of varieties. We also have whales; they are considered the best food. There are other kinds of marine animals that we also use. There are not many people on Kodiak and the other islands. They are called Aleuts; they are humble and very poor. Many speak Russian; they are friendly to us and we know many of them. The mainland is over forty versts[153] to the north from us. Further to the east are other tribes, with names such as the Kenai, Chugach, Kalosh, and others. We know many of them fairly well.

Those of us from Valaam, of which you know three, do not live together: Father Athanasius lives twenty-six or more miles from the church on Afognak Island, which is separated from Kodiak Island by a narrow strait; Father Joseph, your former novice whom you mentioned, lives in the Harbor by the church, in the same small house I mentioned above, for the protection of the library and vestry. On Sundays he conducts the church services along with several boys from the school.

I live about almost seven miles from the Harbor on a separate small island, the name of which is New Valaam. Near by me there is a very small brook; there is enough fish in it in the summer. I live alone. Only about 1.3 miles away there is a family of three Americans; when I am in need, they help me with great love.

Father Joseph often visits me on the small American leather boats, which are locally called *baidarkas*. We have gardens together and share everything. The Americans who live near me consider us natives and help us in everything.

And now only us three are still alive, thanks to the Almighty God. Despite all our sad circumstances and adventures, we joyfully and peacefully live alone. The only sorrow is how to gain our Heavenly Homeland, for which cause we ask and implore you, venerable fathers, kind *batiushkas,* to help us wretches by your holy prayers—in hope of which, I remain

The obedient servant and diligent novice of

Your Reverence,

Wretched Herman.

I also ask you to give my deepest regards to Father Iakov, the former Ivan Alekseevich, the brother of our monk Joseph, although I have not had the opportunity to meet him personally. Please also greet Gabriel Terent'evich. They give me great joy, for which I thank God.

Wretched Herman.

13 December 1819
America, Kodiak Island[154]

The correspondence lasted until 1823. After this time, owing to a sharp decrease in his vision, Father Herman could no longer write or, probably, read.

Below are excerpts from yet another letter of Father Herman to Ianovskii from June 20, 1820.

Your Honor, Kind Sire, Simeon Ivanovich.

I had the honor to receive your gracious, pleasant, and kind letter with the interesting news and the accompanying package. I offer my most fervent gratitude, but I have nothing more with which to pay.

I thank God Almighty, who has preserved your health, and who has protected you from all unfortunate circumstances on land and at sea, yet Who is showing by countless means still more the path of truth, which by following—we achieve eternal joy; by fulfilling the duty of our existence, we fulfill the will of our Creator, who has made us solely for this one purpose.

Father Herman continues writing about the life of a Christian,

I will relate my views, based on the admonitions of Holy Scripture, to those hungering for and seeking after their heavenly homeland:

Faith and love of Christ make a true Christian; our sins do not hinder our Christianity in the least, according to the words of the Savior Himself. He was pleased to say that He came not to call the righteous, but to save sinners; He said that the joy in heaven over one sinner who repents shall be more than over ninety-nine just persons. Likewise He was pleased to say to Simon the Pharisee about the fornicator who was touching His feet, that many debts are forgiven to those who have love, but that those who do not have love are held accountable even for little debts. By these arguments a Christian must bring himself to hope and joy, and by no means heed the darts of despair—to do this requires the shield of faith.

Sin, to one who loves God, is nothing other than an arrow from the enemy in the battle. The true Christian is a soldier, who is forcing his way through the regiments of the invisible enemy to his heavenly homeland. In the words of the Apostle, our homeland is in the heavens, and about battle he says, *For we wrestle not against flesh and blood, but against principalities, against powers.*[155]

The empty desires of this age distance us from our homeland; love for those empty desires and the habit of adorning our soul as if in a foul dress, the apostles call this—the outer man. We, wandering in the journey of this life, calling on God for help, must remove that foulness and put on new desires—a new love for the future age—and through that we must recognize our approach or retreat from our heavenly homeland.

But this is impossible to do quickly, and we must follow the example of the sick, who desiring good health, do not cease searching for the means to heal themselves. I am speaking unclearly, in an utter rush; a lack of time limits me, but I hope that you, with the sharpness of your mind and your burning desire for our good heavenly homeland, can open the path to holy truth not only for yourself, but for others as well. . . .

Glory to holy providences of the merciful God!

With His unfathomable providence He has now shown me a new phenomenon, which I had not seen after living here on Kodiak twenty-five years. Soon after Pascha one young woman, not more than twenty-five years of age, who is able to speak Russian well and who did not know me at all before and never saw me, came to me and heard about the Incarnation of the Son of God and about eternal life. She became so inflamed with love to Jesus Christ that she has no desire to leave me. Her fervent requests convinced me to accept her, against my inclinations and my love for solitude, without regard for what kind of obstacles or difficulties I suggested to her.

And now she has lived with me for more than a month and is not bored. Looking at her with great surprise, I understand the words of the Savior "thou hast hid these things from the wise and prudent, and hast revealed them unto babes."[156] After seeing at her, there are already other female volunteers, but then there is the only issue: I have no strength to build any sort of common residence for them. There are also many young male volunteers, but there is no space.[157]

This woman was called Sof'ia Vlasova. Wrangell wrote of her:

One woman, an Aleut, the wife of a Russian *promyshlennik,* stopped by Father Herman's hut once to find out from a man who had recently arrived from Nushagak about her husband, who had been driven away to there. She had to hear a short sermon from Herman, as it was his habit not to let anyone leave without having said a few words about religion; his words were deeply engraved in her imagination. She was of a loose behavior and felt the pangs of her conscience for the first time.

Having returned home, her former life seemed unbearable to her and soon she again went to Herman and announced her decisive intention to stay with him and to seek her salvation. Herman was already old (60 years). Having overcome his initial shock at this unexpected event and having made peace with the idea of living with a woman in his approaching old age, he accepted her and subsequently built a special small house for her on the seashore. Sof'ia learned to read and to write Russian in a year. And she spoke Russian well. Several orphans—girls from Aleuts and Creoles—soon joined this woman, Sof'ia. Under the guidance of Father Herman she became their instructor, expanding the garden and training them to be hard working. In 1831 I found the garden in a flourishing state and the girl orphans with a healthy appearance; by their open, happy features they showed that they were satisfied with their conditions.[158]

After some time some disciples gathered around Father Herman. As has already been mentioned, the first of them was the orphan Gerasim Ivanovich Zyrianov

(1817–1869). Then there was the Kodiak Aleut Ignatius Alig-iaga (1798–1874) and others. The elder's disciples lived in the guesthouse, which was located close to his cell. Not far from them there stood a house on the shore in which Sof'ia Vlasova and her charges lived. In the period of 1820–1834, there were twelve orphans in all. Those that were not inclined to a life of solitude left New Valaam. The descendants of Ignatius Alig-iaga live in Old Harbor on Kodiak Island to this day.

The priest S. Liashevskii wrote,

> The Russian proverb says, "It is not the order of the church, but to bring order to the orphan." And so Venerable Herman brought order to orphans. Not only did he work with his own hands for them, but asked and cajoled the directors of the colony to give supplies to support the orphanage and the school. It might seem that such a lover of solitude and asceticism as venerable Herman would not be interested in the painstaking cares and concerns of children: to teach, to raise, to feed, and to clothe them. But, as we see, the elder did this with great love, recalling that the Savior Himself loved children and said, "Be like children." . . .
>
> It is not enough to love children; they need to be cared for both physically and spiritually, which the elder did. By the example of his own life, he instructed others to do likewise and even taught them the law of God, raising them from the start in goodness and truth, a feast that is the greatest of arts. "I put the person who can mold the soul of a child higher than a sculptor, higher than any artist," states St John Chrysostom.[159]

Four miles along the shore or 1.3 miles directly from New Valaam was the Aleut village of Ouzinkie. In 1819, three families of Kodiak Aleuts lived there, subsequently there were five families. Many wanted to live closer to Father Herman on Spruce Island. Father Herman taught his disciples the law of God and church singing. He gathered the Aleuts for prayers in his chapel on Sundays and feast days. His disciple Gerasim read the hours and prayers there, while he read the Epistle and Gospel readings himself. He instructed the Aleuts with sermons. The girl orphans sang, with great compunction.

Father Herman enjoyed unquestioned authority with the local residents. Ianovskii wrote,

> Aleuts of both genders and children often visited him: for advice, with complaints of oppression, asking for his help, and with their various needs. Sometimes they bring him fish and help him in his work. He always sorted things out for them; he reconciled them and helped them however he could. On Sundays and feast days, many visited him to pray. Father Herman read the hours, the Epistle, the Gospel, sang, and instructed. He provided the children with rusks or baked pretzels. Children loved him very much, and he loved them as well.[160]

He sorted out their family disputes as well. If he was not able to reconcile a husband and wife, then he permitted them to live apart temporarily. Father Herman explained the necessity of such a measure in this way: "It is better to let them live apart, so that they not fight and quarrel, or else, believe me—it is scary; if they are not separated, there have been instances that the husband killed the wife, or that the wife tormented the husband."

Below is the letter of the Kodiak Aleut Makar Govorukhin, who asked Father Herman for permission to divorce.

Your Reverence, *Batiushka*, Father Herman.

During my time in Pavlovskaia Harbor, after my arrival by *baidarka* from Konstantinovskaia Fort, I intentionally came for my lawful wife who had left me and whom I was trying to persuade to go with me to Nuchek. But she objected to my desire, which is why I am informing you of this. Perhaps in time she will change her intentions, so that in that case, I ask you to give her permission and to exert your efforts for her coming to me when there is an opportunity. But if she does not want to, then I ask that in such a case you not consider me at fault, since I left her to her own will. But I, for my own part, always wish that she would live with me and not unlawfully. However, I submit to your will.

The devoted servant of your Reverence, kind Sire,

The American Marak Govorukhin

From June 12, 1820, Pavlovskaia Harbor.[161]

In 1820, Matvei Ivanovich Murav'ev became the main ruler of Russian America. He arrived at Kodiak in 1818 on the sloop *Kamchatka* and was among the officers who had met with Father Herman. From his letters, it is evident that the elder made an enormous impression on

Murav'ev. As a result, on November 5, 1820, two months after his arrival in Alaska, he wrote to Father Herman:

> Venerable Father!
>
> I flatter myself with the hope that I have not been blotted out of your memory yet, since I had the pleasure during my stay on the frigate *Kamchatka* in Pavloskaia Harbor to receive your blessing. At that time I did not think that fate would bring me to the wild shores of America again or that I would have to spend several difficult years living here. But this has happened and I am left to fulfill my duties with faith in God, hope in Providence, and love to people. As soon as I arrived in Sitka, I found almost famine! And so *Batiushka* . . . [blank in the office copy of the letter], that a fatal path not be offered to me, and for this reason I have need both of advice and your blessing. I hope that you will not abandon me to one or to the other, just as you did not abandon my predecessor [Ianovskii].
>
> I will be on Kodiak continuously in the spring, and then, esteemed father, I hope to give you report of my efforts and to make use of your advice. I entrust myself to your favorable disposition and I ask you to convey my respect to all the brotherhood, to bless my good intentions, and to not neglect to sometimes remember in your prayers that I be enlightened with the wisdom of the wise . . . [unintelligible] and that I be fortified by strength . . . [one word unintelligible].
>
> I remain yours, venerable father . . . and so on.[162]

Murav'ev tried to support Father Herman in any way he could. He collected donations in New Arkhangel'sk to help the orphans. Another letter of his to Father Herman has been preserved:

> Venerable Father Herman!
>
> On Kodiak last year you had a contagion. Thank the Lord, it ended; its consequences continue. Many poor orphans remain and . . . [unintelligible] God to not abandon them, and kind people remembered. By voluntary subscription they gathered some funds here, with which they purchased these things that I send to you. I ask you to distribute them according to your conscience and your kind heart; help the poor, who are as unknown to me personally as they are known to you. Do not give an account of this to anyone, except to God and to your conscience. And do not withhold your blessing from us,
>
> Venerable Father,
>
> I remain your humble servant.
>
> A list of items follows: 3 pieces gray soldier's cloth, 3 packages broadcloth, 1 duck cloth, 259 1.2-*arshin*[163] burlap, 1,000 needles.[164]

The following letter serves as yet one more piece of evidence of the love of locals for Father Herman.

> Your Reverence, most-kind Sire,
>
> Father Herman.
>
> The children of your fatherly blessing Ivan and Elena, falling at the feet of your reverence, ask for your blessing in absentia and for your holy prayers for us, sinners.

And about myself I can relate that, after this trip, we remain alive and safe, by your prayers, and henceforth we rely on the power of God and on your prayers; we ask that in the future by your Fatherly mercy, you not cease your prayers to the saints, so that the Lord direct our life by His blessing and by His word not abandon us sinners.

We ask that you not be angry now—there is not a thing to send to you; there have been no ships, just one Englishman Mick, our acquaintance and friend. The Company has entered into a contract with him, that he supply everything necessary for the Company here [to Kodiak]; we gave him money and a list of what we need. He will return back here from Canton in March, perhaps even earlier. The vessel *Kutuzov* is also expected here from Petersburg.

If we will be alive, then we will certainly thank you for that. Having written this to you, we, Ivan and Elena Shchukin, bow down most humbly and affectionately, June 21, 1821.[165]

As mentioned in the letter, Ivan Matveevich and Elena Shchukin were Russian "settlers," exiled for some crime to Siberia. In 1794, they were sent to America, where Ivan worked as a metalsmith. They were given permission to return to Russia in 1823.

Monk Joseph visited his spiritual father often. When he fell seriously ill, he moved over to Father Herman on Spruce Island, where he died in 1823 at the age of 50.

The Kodiak Aleuts loved to listen to the instruction of Father Herman and often visited him from Kodiak and other places. The elder's spiritual talks were fascinating, and they had a remarkable influence on the listeners. Father Herman was loquacious: he spoke wisely, practically, and instructively. Most of all he spoke about eternity, about the salvation of the soul, and about the life of the future age. He recounted much from the Prologue and from the lives of the saints.

Not only people sought to interact with Father Herman, but animals as well. They did not fear him at all. The elder always fed birds with fish; a multitude of them took up residence near his cell. A tame ermine lived under his cell. This is very dangerous little creature that always flees from people, but the elder could feed him by hand. Others observed him feeding bears, who showed no aggressiveness. All living things obtained a peaceful disposition from contact with the elder.

Having completely devoted himself to the service of God, caring solely about the glorification of His All-Holy Name, living a long way from his homeland, enduring a multitude of offenses and hardships, spending decades in exalted ascetic struggles of self-denial—in all of this Father Herman was deemed worthy of many supernatural gifts from God.

He gave the sick water that had been blessed on the Feast of Theophany, and this medicine always brought relief. Once Sof'ia wanted to go to another island with her girls to gather seaweed. It was Sunday, and the elder told them, "You should not go today, but tomorrow." They discussed among themselves that there had been no good weather all week and that only God knew whether the next day would be good. They left without the elder's blessing. When they had traveled a good distance from the shore, their *baidarka* ran into an underwater rock that tore a hole in the leather skin of the *baidarka*. One of the girls drowned.

Upon their return, the elder called them over and said, "This is what it means to be disobedient and contradictory!" They fell to their knees and asked forgiveness. The elder forgave them and said, "When I went to the seashore in the morning, on that very same spot I saw a man, sitting on the rock and stirring the water with his hand. He was very ugly."[166]

Once there was flooding on Spruce Island. Alarmed, the residents ran to Father Herman's cell. He took an icon of the Mother of God from his disciples' house, brought it out, placed it on the seashore, and began to pray. After the prayer, he told those present, "Do not fear; the water will not go further than this place where the holy icon stands." The flooding immediately ceased. Then, promising the exact same help in the future—through the intercessions of the Most-Holy Directress, he instructed his disciple Sof'ia to place the icon on the shore in the event of high water.

A fire somehow occurred on Spruce Island. Father Herman, along with his disciple Ignatius, drew a line on the ground, removed the moss along it, and said, "Be calm—the fire will not cross this line!" The next day, when there was no hope of escape, the fire reached the line drawn by the elder through the strong force of the wind. It ran along it and stopped, not touching the thick forest located across the line.[167]

In 1823, the priest Frumentii Mordovskii arrived in Alaska. In July of 1824, Father Frumentii was assigned to Kodiak, where without authorization he began to act as the head of the local church. In the spring of 1825, Father Frumentii demanded that the manager of the Kodiak company office, S. Ia. Nikiforov, accompany him to Spruce Island to conduct a search of Father Herman's cell. He valued all the property, including the chapel, at 8,000 rubles. This sum included money, about 1,500 rubles in cash and assignats.[168] Father Herman had kept this money for the construction of a new church on Kodiak, because the existing one had become extremely dilapidated by that time.

It was later recounted that during the search the *pro-myshlennik* Ponomar'kov began to pull up the floorboards with an ax. Looking at him, Father Herman said, "My friend, you have taken that ax in vain—it will deprive you of your life!" Ponomar'kov was shortly sent to the Nikolaevskii redoubt on the Kenai Peninsula, where, while sleeping, Indians cut his head off with an ax.

Father Frumentii ordered Father Herman to abandon Spruce Island and took him to Kodiak. When news of the search, the list of property, and the transfer of St

Herman to Pavlovskaia Harbor reached Murav'ev, he immediately ordered the office manager, Nikiforov, to begin an investigation. Father Frumentii was required to prove that he had acted with the blessing of Church authorities. Murav'ev also had the Central Administration of the RAC in St Petersburg direct an inquiry to the Most-Holy Synod of the Russian Orthodox Church about Father Frumentii's authority.

Incidentally, Hieromonk Athanasius also endured persecution. If the property of St Herman was recorded at least in the presence of the Kodiak office manager, then Father Athanasius was not even present himself during the inventory of his property. On April 25, Chief Manager Murav'ev informed the Okhotsk office in disbelief, "Beyond my expectations, Hieromonk Athanasius has been sent with the brig *Kiakhta*, which came from Kodiak [to New Arkhangel'sk] for departure to Irkutsk by the priest Frumentii."[169] Murav'ev sent Father Athanasius to Russia. Having arrived in Okhotsk, Father Athanasius departed for Irkutsk, where he arrived "ailing both in body and spirit." There he announced that he wanted to reveal something secret to the members of the Most-Holy Synod.

They called him to St Petersburg, where he announced that over the past twenty-five years the population of Kodiak Island had shrunk from 7,000 to 4,000 because "the Russian American Company, conducting hunts for animals and other business near Kodiak and in other parts of America, has sent workers of the Christian faith to distant places for ten years at a time and longer. For such a significant period of time people remain separated from their wives and children, do not have priests with them, and are deprived of any instruction in the faith."[170] Father Athanasius was allocated a pension of 200 rubles a year and assigned to Valaam Monastery, where he died in 1831.

At the initiative of Murav'ev, Father Mordovskii was removed, but owing to difficulties in communication and a lengthy investigation, he was only sent out of Alaska under the new Chief Manager Wrangell in 1832. His replacement, the priest Aleksii Sokolov, was transferred from New Arkhangel'sk the next year.

Father Herman also endured many woes and temptations from demons. His disciple Gerasim once entered the elder's cell without saying the typical prayer; he did not receive an answer to any of his questions to Father Herman. The next day, he asked the elder the reason for his silence the previous day. Father Herman answered, "When I arrived on this island and settled in this deserted place, demons came to me many times in human and animal form as if for some necessity. I often endured various offenses and temptations from them, so that now I do not speak to those who enter my cell without a prayer."[171]

Basil Ivanovich Kashevarov, the merchant son of the St Petersburg Province, became the next manager of the Kodiak office of the RAC in 1830. His wife, Eugenia, was the daughter of a priest, Father Aleksei. Father Herman established a close relationship with him. Kashevarov often visited the elder on Spruce Island, and sometimes the elder traveled to him on Kodiak.

Kashevarov was a very strict, but fair, manager. He would often severely punish the guilty, and so only Father Herman could defend the accused. He often persuaded Kashevarov to forgive the guilty by saying that as a result he would also be forgiven in the next life.

Also in 1830, Captain First-Class Baron Ferdinand Peterovich Wrangell became the new chief manager in Russian America. Father Herman met with him twice, in 1831 and 1834.

Wrangell wrote,

> In his faith, Father Herman is Orthodox, to which he is devoted without any deception or deceit. Being gifted with a quick mind and a sharp memory, his thoughts, so to speak, run rampant among the Bible, Sacred History, and the Penances, which he knows almost by heart. And although poor vision has kept him from writing or reading anything for more than ten years, his memory finds in the aforementioned writings a vast reservoir for discussion and conversation, of which he never becomes exhausted and which pours forth from him with quick speech, despite his old age.
>
> To appearances he is a Cynic:[172] he not only does not care about the cleanliness of his dress or linens, but does not even wash himself. He is of a cheerful disposition, loves to

laugh at the humorous, and participates in all secular events, particularly historic ones. At the same time he does not speak for long about these subjects, and, finally, moves without fail to his topic—to religion.

On Spruce Island he has found the solitude and serene existence to which he has striven his whole life. Earlier on Kodiak, he had to withstand and endure clashes with people of a kind whom, in all probability, he would never have met in Russia. . . . He drank the cup of suffering which was allotted to him, and then received his award in his utterly calm disposition. He did not seek honors, since he refused many offers, which would have been accepted by a man in search of a higher place in society.[173]

Wrangell wrote about Father Herman's disciple Sof'ia and his "agricultural school":

In 1831 I found agriculture in full bloom. The girl orphans looked healthy and their open, happy features showed that they were satisfied with their condition.

Then I ordered the office to protect Herman, to build him a chapel, and to help in other ways. This was done; his place is called New Valaam. In 1834 Sof'ia had five girls (two left on their own, having sinned against the chastity which was required of them). Five Aleut families have moved not far from them, who quickly settled in and, having received help from Valaam, also lent them a hand. On Valaam they gather up to 120 barrels of potatoes; they grow turnips, garlic, cabbage, and carrots. Sof'ia and the girls work from morning till night. They sew, weave baskets, and help with the farming. They have ten head of livestock. I tried earnestly to convince and to ask Father Herman to strengthen the girls in religion, and—having taught them farming, and being used to working—to have them marry, after having found a good man in the Aleut settlements and having settled close to him. But all my efforts were in vain. He maintains a monastic rule, and those who do not want to remain virgins have to leave Valaam.[174]

On his last visit to Spruce Island, Wrangell wrote, at Father Herman's dictation, a will that was sent to the Central Administration of the RAC in St Petersburg. Then he asked Wrangell to send him an icon of the Meeting of the Lord[175] from Russia. Wrangell fulfilled this request. An icon with a silver setting was brought to New Arkhangel'sk. From there, the new Chief Manager Ivan Antonovich Kupreianov sent it from there to New Valaam not long before the elder's death.

Father Herman also asked Wrangell about assistance for Baranov's widow, the Kodiak Aleut Anna Grigor'evna Rasskazchikova, who had moved to Spruce Island and was in great need. Wrangell also fulfilled this request.

The new ruler Kupreianov treated the holy elder with great respect. He visited Kodiak and Spruce Islands in the summer of 1836. In accordance with a request of Father Herman, Kupreianov ordered that a former *promyshlennik* of German extraction, surnamed Riuppe, be assigned teacher in the orphan school at New Valaam as help for the elder. Many years later, at the start of the twentieth century, "Old Man Riuppe" (it is unknown whether this was his son or grandson) lived alone on Spruce Island carefully tending the grave of Venerable Herman.

Two surviving letters of Kupreianov to the elder testify to his reverential treatment of Father Herman.

Pious Father Herman!

Not having had the pleasure to know you personally, I consider it my responsibility to attest to you that I am filled with the utmost respect for your lengthy, useful, and God-pleasing life in the Colonies. I ask God to lengthen your days and you, to not forget me in your prayers, that the Lord may bless and direct my activities for the good of the Colonies. Likewise, I introduce my wife, Iuliia Ivanovna and our newborn son, Iakov. I have a strong desire and soon hope both to see you personally, and to take your blessing. In the event of any kind of need, do not hesitate, holy Father, to write me candidly about whatever concerns you; be certain of my sincerity just as of my total respect to you, which I always retain.

Pious Father!

Your devoted servant, Ivan Kupreianov.

3 March 1836[176]

Pious Father Herman!

During the stay of my predecessor, Baron Ferdinand Peterovich Wrangell, on Kodiak in 1834, you asked him to send an icon of the Meeting of the Lord from Russia for your chapel on New Valaam. Along with this you asked about assistance to the Aleut Anna, who lives under your care and who once lived for a long time with the former Chief Manager Baranov and is the mother of his children.

I make haste to inform you, pious Father, that the Central Administration of the Company in reply to the corresponding declaration of my predecessor, of 12 March of this year, informs me that, by your request, it is sending you through the New Arkhangel'sk Office the requested icon in a silver setting. Concerning the aforementioned Aleut Anna, after consulting with the former Chief Manager, Captain Second-Class Ianovskii, it has come to this determination: that the New Arkhangel'sk Office would transfer funds every year for this Aleut Anna to the Kodiak Office or would send the items and provisions necessary for her, purchased with these funds from the Sitka Store, directly to Kodiak in her name; the appropriate order from me about this has been issued.

Informing you about this, I consider it necessary to add, that I ordered the Manager of the Kodiak Office Kashevarov to dispatch to you the man, named Riuppe as I recall, whom you personally requested this summer, when the number of charges I intend will be assembled on Spruce Island.

I have heard, unfortunately, that the condition of your health is not better since we saw each other; I would be pleased to hear of the restoration of your strength.

My whole family wishes you health and a long life. As always, I remain most respectfully yours.

Pious Father,

Your devoted servant, Ivan Kupreianov

To Pious Father Herman. 16 October 1836[177]

Father Herman had the gift of clairvoyance and could foretell the future. As was noted during his meeting with Wrangell in 1834, the latter wrote a letter that the elder dictated because Father Herman himself could no longer write. When the letter was written and read aloud, Father Herman congratulated the baron with the rank of admiral, which he was about to receive. In October 1835, Wrangell passed affairs to the new chief manager and left for Russia, to St Petersburg, where he arrived in June 1836. In July, he had already received the rank of rear-admiral.

The Creole Konstantine Larionov, remembering this incident in 1867, wrote, "When Wrangell left for St Petersburg, then that prediction came true! Perhaps this good man is still prospering and has not forgotten what has happened."[178]

It is likely that Father Herman went completely blind by 1835. In the last years of his life, he led a very secretive and solitary life. He let no one into his cell and left it very rarely. Father Herman devoted all his time to the ascetic struggles of prayer, fasting, and self-denial.

CHAPTER 4

Father Herman's Repose and His Legacy

Shortly before his death, Father Herman told his disciples,

> When I die, bury me beside Father Joseph. Immediately kill my ox; he has served me enough. Bury me yourselves and do not speak of my death in the harbor; the people in the harbor will not see my face. Don't send for a priest and do not wait for him—don't wait! Do not wash my body; place it on a board; fold my hands on my chest; wrap me in my mantia and cover my face with its wings and my head with my klobuk. Whosoever wishes to bid me farewell, let them kiss the cross; do not show my face to anyone. Having lowered me into the ground, cover me with my former blanket.[179]

As has already been mentioned, *blanket* refers to the board beneath which the elder slept.

When Father Herman felt that the time of his departure was approaching, he ordered his disciple Gerasim to light candles before the icons and to read the Acts of the Holy Apostles. After a certain period of time, his face lit up, and he said loudly, "Glory to Thee, O Lord!" He ordered the reading to stop and announced that it was pleasing to the Lord that He extend his life for one more week.

In a week, the candles were again lit, and the same Gerasim read the Acts of the Holy Apostles. The elder quietly bowed his head, the cell filled with a pleasant fragrance, and Father Herman passed away. Thus did he blessedly depart with the sleep of the righteous in the eighty-sixth year of his life, on November 15, 1836.

On that same night, the residents of the village Katana, which is located on the island of Afognak, saw an unusual column of light over Spruce Island extending from earth to heaven. Astounded by this miraculous occurrence, the Creole Gerasim Vologdin and his wife Anna said, "Evidently, Father Herman has left us," and they began to pray. Likewise, the Kodiak Aleut Anna Hatsmyshknak saw this column of light. Konstantine Larionov wrote about this in 1867: "I heard about this from many people, who saw it from various places; others saw it at sea, while paddling in *baidarkas*."[180]

For some reason, the disciples of the elder did not immediately kill his ox. The ox began to languish; on the next day, from a running start, it knocked its forehead into a tree and fell dead.

Despite the dying wishes of Father Herman, his disciples decided not to bury him without informing the authorities in the village of Pavlovskaia Harbor. The disciple, sent with the sad news to Kodiak, reported that Kashevarov, the manager of the Kodiak RAC office, forbade the burial of the elder before his arrival. He ordered that the best coffin be made for the departed and prepared to personally bring it immediately to Spruce Island along with the local priest, Father Aleksii Sokolov.

Such instructions were against the will of the departed; so a terrible wind blew, rain poured, and an awful storm began. Despite the fact that the crossing from Pavlovskaia Harbor to Spruce Island took only two hours, no one resolved to enter the sea in such weather. The storm lasted for a whole month, and all that time the body of Father Herman lay in a warm house, but not even the slightest odor came from him, and his face remained just as it had been in life.

Finally, after a month, the experienced *promyshlennik* Koz'ma Uchilishchev (1793–1861) was able to bring the coffin from Pavlovskaia Harbor. He was the only person who had come from Kodiak. The residents of Spruce Island alone committed the remains of the elder to the earth on December 13. Thus, the last will of Father Herman was fulfilled. After the burial of the venerable one, the wind immediately abated and the surface of the sea became smooth as a mirror.

Documents concerning the date of the repose of Father Herman are mentioned in the article of N. I. Ponomareva. The directors of the RAC wrote to the Irkutsk Archbishop Innocent in 1841:

> The Central Administration of the Russian-American Company, having received a dispatch from the Chief Manager of the Russian-American colony, the Guard's Crew Captain of the First-Rank Kupreianov, dated 5 May of this year, No. 137, about the death of the monk Herman, which happened 15 November last year, 1836, consider it our responsibility to most respectfully inform Your Eminence of this fact.
>
>   Director Ivan Prokof'ev.
>   Director Nicholas Kusov.
>   Office Manager Bazhenov."[181]

The metrical book of Holy Resurrection Church at Pavlovskaia Harbor on Kodiak Island contains the following about the burial of Father Herman: "In December, on the thirteenth day, the member of the spiritual mission, monk Herman, 76 years old,[182] from paralysis, buried on Valaam Island."[183]

It is known that among St Herman's disciples, Gerasim Zyrianov, Ignatius Alig-iaga, and Sof'ia Vlasova were present at his repose.

Zyrianov, who was nineteen years old in 1836, stayed living on Spruce Island. In 1842, he met with Bishop Innocent (Veniaminov) during his visit to Spruce Island.

At the recommendation of the bishop, he was taken to serve in church in Pavlovskaia Harbor. A year later, the priest of this church, Father Peter Litvintsev,[184] wrote Bishop Innocent a letter on October 4, 1843:

At Your Grace's behest, the Creole Gerasim Zyrianov, who was taken from Spruce Island to the Kodiak church for instruction, has during the course of the year shown himself to be zealous, humble, and reliable. He has securely memorized the expanded catechesis; he has learned reading, singing, and the order of services; he could be a good clergyman. Throughout the year, the Creole Zyrianov earned his keep with his relative, the steward Silin. Now that same steward Silin intends to leave for Russia and Gerasim Zyrianov will be deprived of his assistance.

Therefore I have been so bold as to suggest to Your Grace: would it not be fitting to accept the Creole Gerasim Zyrianov as a sacristan of the Kodiak church, and assign him the wage which the departed sacristan, the Creole Philip Friukov, had received here, that is, 240 rubles a year. I intercede for the above-mentioned Creole, an orphan of archpastoral mercy.[185]

The appeal was approved, and in 1844 Zyrianov became sacristan. In addition to his responsibilities, Zyrianov and the sacristan Il'ia Ivanovich Tyzhnov, a graduate of the Irkutsk seminary, spent a year and a half translating Scripture into the language of the Kodiak Aleuts. In April 1845, the latter wrote a report to Bishop Innocent:

By my own choice, I have taken upon myself the task of learning the Kodiak Aleut language since 1841. With thanks to God, I now have the joy to inform Your Grace that I, with God's help, have learned the Kodiak Aleut language as well as I could and have translated prayers, Ecclesiastical history, catechesis, and the Gospel of Matthew, as well composing a primer—all of these translations are ready. I have grammar notes about the Kodiak Aleut language and a dictionary of this language in Russian in draft form, but have not completed them.

Informing Your Grace of my translations, I also have the responsibility to inform you of who, in particular, provided assistance in this project. The Kodiak Aleut Koz'ma Uchilishchev first gave me some understanding of the language. After him the sacristan of the Kodiak church Gerasim Zyrianov (Creole) clarified my understanding of the language and over the course of a year and a half translated with me.

Bishop Innocent put this resolution on the report: "To the sacristan Gerasim Zyrianov as an award for his labors to issue him once the sum of two hundred rubles assignats[186] from the General Fund of the American Church and to the Aleut Koz'ma Uchilishchev, forty rubles."[187]

Zyrianov, however, did not remain sacristan for long. Some conflict arose between him and the priest Peter Litvintsev; the latter submitted a report, and January 2, 1846, Zyrianov was removed from the Ecclesiastical Department. He was only informed of the firing on October 30, about which he gave a signed statement:

I, the undersigned, give this written statement to the Ecclesiastical Administration as a testament to the fact that I will not
call myself a minor cleric under any circumstances and will
also not consider myself a member of the Ecclesiastical Department. To wit, I sign by my own hand.

The one who is removed from Ecclesiastical status
The Creole Gerasim Zyrianov[188]

Meanwhile in the fall of 1846, Il'ia Tyzhnov left
for St Petersburg to enter the Ecclesiastical Academy.
He published his translations in the capital. In 1847,
The Guide of a Christian[189] was issued, and in 1848, *The
Aleut-Kodiak Dictionary*[190] and *The Gospel of the Apostle
Matthew*.[191]

These books reached Kodiak in 1849. Bishop Innocent
wrote, "Last year, a book written in Kodiak appeared, and
there is no doubt but that that they will serve to spread
first, knowledge of prayers among the people there, and
then, knowledge of the Law and the Faith. The priest
there said that in one place, in his presence, the natives
shed tears of compunction at hearing the prayer for the
first time in their own language; this is especially notable
since those natives rarely cry."[192]

In 1848, Zyrianov married an eighteen-year-old girl,
Maria Bruseninaia, and shortly thereafter returned to
Spruce Island, where he moved into Sof'ia Vlasova's
house. By 1850, he had restored St Herman's old chapel,
which had been built in 1832 on orders from Wrangell.

There he conducted services, consoling the laity: he read prayers, baptized newborns, and buried the departed.

By 1868, the Zyrianovs already had seven children. On August 20, 1869, at the age of 52, Gerasim Ivanovich Zyrianov died a sudden death. Four days later two of his sons, the twins Peter and Paul, died of poisoning.[193]

G. I. Khol'mberg mentions one of Father Herman's disciples. He wrote,

> When I visited Spruce Island in 1851, I stopped there [in New Valaam]. A Kodiak woman named Maria lived there at the current time. She was unhappy in her married life. Because of this, she moved to Father Herman, who taught her to read and write. She took care of him until he died. Although she is already over sixty, she conducts every Sunday service in the chapel that Father Herman had built; these services are attended by the Russians and Creoles of the island. The people in the colonies consider her to be almost a saint. In spite of this, there are rumors now, as there were earlier, that her relationship with Father Herman, evidently, was not completely ideal.[194]

In all likelihood, this was written about Sof'ia Vlasova.

In the middle of the 1860s, the Kodiak priest Peter Kashevarov visited his grave. He saw the wooden grave marker, which Father Herman's disciples had erected. "I saw it myself and now am able to say that it is not in the least touched by time, as if it had been assembled today."[195] It was also seen in 1896 by the then Hieromonk Anatoly

(Kamenskii); he ended his days as archbishop of Irkutsk in the torture chambers of the GPU.[196] Archimandrite Gerasim (Schmaltz) saw the same marker during his first visit to Spruce Island in 1927.

After the death of the elder, his prophecies began to come true one after the other. For example, he said, "After my death there will be an epidemic, and many people will die from it, and the Russians will combine the Aleuts."[197]

In fact, in the winter of 1835, an epidemic of small-pox began in the capital city of Russian America, New Arkhangel'sk, on the island of Sitka. It spread from the south to the north among the population of the Pacific Ocean shore of North America. In New Arkhangel'sk, the entire population received vaccinations, yet the Indians living in the village closest to the capital refused the shots. Only a few people died from smallpox in New Arkhangel'sk, while in the Indian village half the population—around 350 people—perished.

Smallpox appeared on Kodiak in June 1837, when a flu epidemic was already raging. The epidemic ended in January 1838. In all, 738 people from the Kodiak Archipelago died, despite the fact that the RAC tried to save people with smallpox vaccinations. This mortality represented a very large percentage of the total number of the Aleut population. In 1830, before the spread of smallpox, the total population of the Kodiak Archipelago was 2,501, not counting those Aleuts who lived in various RAC villages from California to the Kyril Islands.

In May 1840, A. K. Etolin became the new chief manager of Russian America. By his orders, over the course of 1840–1842, all the local population of Kodiak and the neighboring islands were combined into seven villages: Three Hierarchs, Afognak, Karulia, Orlov, Chinia on the island Lesna, Agekhtalik, and Akkhiok. This reform did not affect the residents of settlements more distant from Kodiak: Katmai on the Alaskan peninsula and Ukamok on the island of the same name. The settlement of Ouzinkie on Spruce Island had earlier been turned into a village for pensioners of the RAC; several Kodiak Aleut families also resided there.

In 1835, a son was born to the manager of the Kodiak office, Kashevarov; he was baptized March 25 with name Aleksii. Taking the infant from the font, Father Herman told him, "I pity you, dear *kum*,[198] being replaced will be unpleasant for you." In 1838, Kashevarov was accused of financial abuses and, while being replaced, was tied up and sent to New Arkhangel'sk.[199]

Father Herman often said that America would soon have its own hierarch, at a time when no one even thought about this. In Alaska in the 1830s, there were only four priests—one each in New Arkhangel'sk, on Kodiak Island, on Unalaska Island, and on Atka Island—and one monk—Father Herman himself on Spruce Island. It is clear that at that time there was no hope that America would soon have its own hierarch. But in 1840, only a few years later, by the will of God, the Kamchatka, Kyril, and

Aleut Diocese was formed, the head of which became Bishop Innocent (Veniaminov). Before being tonsured as a monk, he was the priest John, who had served on Unalaska Island.

Father Herman once told his disciple the Kodiak Aleut Ignatius Alig-iaga, "Thirty years will pass after my death and all those now living on Spruce Island will perish. You will be left to live alone and will be old and poor and then you will remember me."

Ignatius wrote, "It is amazing that a man like us could know all of this such a long time in advance! Nevertheless, he is not a typical man! He saw our thoughts and unwittingly led us so that we revealed them to him and received guidance!" This prediction, as with many others, came to pass exactly. Ignatius Alig-iaga died in 1874; he was the last resident of Spruce Island to have known Father Herman.

Valaam Monastery remembered about Father Herman again in 1864. That was when the pilgrim Grigorii Michaelovich Lazarev visited Valaam. A member of the lower middle class from Tsarskoe Selo, he had lived in America for more than ten years. Of those ten, he served in Kodiak from 1855 to 1861. Lazarev told the abbot of the monastery, Hegumen Damascene, information about the elder that he himself had heard from his closest disciple, the Creole Gerasim Zyrianov.

Wishing to confirm the information he had received, as well as to learn details about the life of Father Herman,

Hegumen Damascene wrote letters that same year (1864) to Zyrianov, to the vicar of the Kamchatka Diocese, His Grace Peter (Ekaterinovskii), and to the archbishop of Kamchatka and the Aleutian Islands, Innocent (Veniaminov).

In the letter to Archbishop Innocent, he wrote, in part, "Among the other information there is one part which particularly concerns Your Eminence, as if you had related it yourself. It is the following: a fierce storm . . . carried you along the waves in sight of Spruce Island. Everyone was in despair . . . inwardly you asked Father Herman to save you from sinking. Suddenly a favorable wind arose, which shifted back to its previous direction, along your course to the harbor."[200] This letter refers to the voyage of the ship *Kvikhpak* under the command of Skipper Lindenberg from New Arkhangel'sk to Kodiak, which lasted from February 19 to March 18, 1842. At that time, this voyage would have typically taken about a week.[201]

In 1865, Hegumen Damascene received a letter from the city of Kaluga from the former chief manager of the RAC Ianovskii. He wrote that he personally knew "the former monk of the Valaam Monastery, Father Herman, an esteemed holy man, a great ascetic." He also mentioned that he was in possession of two letters, which he kept "as a treasure from the holy elder, my former spiritual guide, the memory of whom is holy for me." A correspondence arose; Ianovskii gave the monastery the two letters from Father Herman, as well relating a series of interesting details about him. About himself, he wrote, "I am an ailing old man of 77 years; I am standing on the edge of the grave—and who knows, perhaps the Lord is extending my life in order to pass on information about the life of the elder."[202]

In 1867, responses to the letters to Bishop Peter and Archbishop Innocent were received in Valaam. No reply was received from the Creole Gerasim Zyrianov.

Archbishop Innocent wrote,

It is correct that in 1842, while sailing to Kodiak, we were at sea for a long time and found ourselves in an extreme situation, since for our 52 passengers less than half barrel of water remained. At the entrance to the Kodiak harbor we were met by a headwind that blew for three days. During this time our ship sailed back and forth, or, in nautical terms, tacked from the southern promontory of Kodiak to Spruce Island, where Father Herman lived and died. On the third day toward the evening, when our ship again approached Spruce Island (for perhaps the twentieth or thirtieth time), I, looking at it, said in my mind, "If you, Father Herman, were pleasing to the Lord, then let the wind be changed." And truly, it seemed, a quarter of an hour did not pass before the wind became favorable and we entered the cove that same night and dropped anchor. . . . Then after a little while I traveled to the grave [of Father Herman] and served a *pannikhida*.[203, 204]

In his travel journal for his review of his diocese, Bishop Innocent wrote,

I consider this voyage of ours, which lasted twenty-eight days, to be one of the most successful voyages in comparison to typical ones due to the results, and in spite of all the difficult circumstances. Despite: first, the time of the year (March is one of the stormiest months of the year); second, the cramped condition of the ship, which reached such an extent that at the start of our trip, that is, when we had a full load, in the ship's hold we could hardly sit one beside the other, which of course would not have been the case if I had not been on the ship with my retinue; third, constant cold and even frost, which was strong, that seawater froze on the deck and on the rigging; fourth, a lack of water, such that at the end the amount was extremely restricted (the total for each day and for all uses was two bottles of water for each sailor; one and a half bottles for passengers); fifth, a lack of rusk, such that near the end despite the most restricted portions, was only sufficient until March 20, despite the fact that the ship's cargo included much flour and salted beef, but without water nothing can be done with them; sixth, the impossibility of being on deck, and, as a result, of getting some air and airing out the hold of the ship with fresh air; and seventh, the decline in spirits of many of the passengers at the lack of hope of reaching the shore due to the constant stiff contrary winds, which threatened to bring disaster if they lasted seven more days. But despite all of this, every last one of those on the ship made it to shore healthy, and no one was sick during the voyage, not even one of the sailors, who by necessity had to stand on the deck several hours at a time without moving. Five days before the end of the voyage, one of the passengers gave birth to a child. Despite the utter lack of all supplies (she was not even allowed to have an extra bottle of water), both she and the child survived.

All this, I consider to be "a visible sign of God's mercy" to us.[205]

This very voyage is described in a letter written by Catherine Ivanovna Petelinaia, the daughter of Archbishop Innocent.

For five days we sailed easily to Spruce Island [actually, Kodiak Island]; there were favorable winds. At night on the fifth day [February 23], strong blows and rocking were felt on the ship; everyone was afraid. There was an earthquake, which lasted a minute or two. Soon fierce contrary winds began to blow freezing air; the sea began to foam and seeth. Wave after wave, fiercely crashing on the vessel, showered down on the deck.

The ship was not large; there were about seventy passengers. All the hatches were tightly boarded up; on deck there was only the crew with its captain and Vladyka. All the other travelers were locked in the hold. For 28 days and nights the fragile ship was tossed by the waves; it was so strong that it was not possible to walk. We crawled on hands and knees or sat motionless; everyone's legs became swollen. It was extremely difficult to endure sitting for 28 days in total darkness, and without food or water. There was not even any rusk; all that remained was some dust from them. There wasn't enough water either; only half a bottle for four people was allowed each day. Finally, when there was no more water, we squeezed it out of the sails and drank it. We boiled salted beef in sea water and gave each passenger a small piece. Everyone was sick. After the stormy weather, the winds finally became more and more calm; the sky cleared and by evening we could see the shore. . . .

Water soon reached the ship along with provisions for the exhausted sailors. Vladyka served a Thanksgiving moleben with bended knees on the deck. He served with such compunction and feeling that all the passengers shed a few tears.[206]

Bishop Peter, having received the letter from Valaam, charged the Kodiak priest Peter Kashevarov and one of the more educated local residents—the Creole Konstantine Andreevich Larionov—to gather information about Father Herman. They gathered all that they knew themselves and that they heard from others. The Kodiak Aleut Ignatius Alig-iaga, a disciple of the elder, provided Larionov with much interesting information. Moreover, while writing about the various miracles of the elder, Larionov mentioned the names of witnesses. Thus, he wrote that Pelagiia Stepanovna, Peter Gavrilov, Basil Gagarin, and Irina Gagarina witnessed the elder's miracle of stopping the flooding. Likewise, in other instances he notes the surname of witnesses.[207]

Thus, by the will of God, thoroughly reliable information about the life of Father Herman was gathered at Valaam. From this information his biography was compiled; it was read to the brotherhood December 13, 1867, the day Father Herman is commemorated. That is, this happened thirty-one years after his death, in accordance with the elder's prophecy. In 1868, this biography had already been published.[208]

Despite the fact that many of Father Herman's predictions came true soon after his death, there were others that have been fulfilled only in our times. For example, he told his disciples, "Although many years will pass after my death, I will not be forgotten and the place where I live will not be empty: a monk like me, fleeing human glory, will come and will live on Spruce Island—and Spruce will not be without people!" This monk was Father Gerasim (Schmaltz), who lived on Spruce Island from 1935 until his death in 1969.

His friend, Father Stephen, tells the story of how St Herman himself called Father Gerasim to Spruce Island.

When Archimandrite Gerasim came to Spruce Island, he did not know if he should move to this genuine Valaam-like wilderness. He received an answer from St Herman: he appeared to him while he was awake, which Father Gerasim told me, as his friend, with whom he had been in correspondence for many years. Perhaps he didn't tell anyone else about this or write it to anyone. This is what Father Gerasim told me himself word for word. He saw with his own eyes in the middle of the day the appearance of a shining, bright St Herman, who was standing between two large spruce trees. At this moment there was a Paschal bell chime, and he clearly heard the words of St Herman: "I am here ringing this Paschal chime," that is, in his heavenly monastery. And the vision ceased. Then Father Gerasim understood, that this is the blessing of Venerable Herman for him to stay there to live forever.[209]

Talking in 1832 with the boy Konstantine Larionov, who was then twelve years old, Father Herman said, "My dear boy, what do you think, will building a chapel be in vain?"

The boy answered, "*Batiushka*, I do not know."

The elder, having been quiet for a little, said, "My child, remember, in time there will be a monastery on this place."

Larionov wrote in 1867, "Until now, I do not know why . . . he favored me with such a prediction or if he foresaw, that in time, although I am unworthy, I will be the one to transmit his words."[210]

All these predictions that were made while the elder was alive were first published in 1868, one year after the sale of Alaska. By this time, a large part of the Russian population had abandoned Alaska; the Orthodox churches had fallen into ruin, and the remaining clergy numbered a few individuals. Larionov also left Alaska; in 1868, he moved to Nikolaevsk-on-the-Amur. Who could have imagined then, that there, on the territory of another government, a monk might take up residence? It was especially difficult at that time to believe the predictions of the elder, but surely he knew that Alaska would always belong to Russia. The priest Liashevskii considered that this phrase from St Herman's letter—"Since this people's state of prosperity has been bestowed for an unknown period of time by Divine Providence into the hands of the resident Russian authorities"—means that the elder knew of the approaching sale of Alaska.[211]

This is how the glory of St Herman began to spread: first the spoken stories of eyewitnesses, and then his biography composed by the Valaam Monastery monks. These have preserved for us unique accounts of the life and miracles of this great ascetic, who became the father of his flock, the Kodiak Aleuts; who showed true Christian love for his neighbor; and who reached amazing heights in prayer and ascetic struggle. The historical documents continue to reveal more and more new facts about this most interesting page in the life of the Russian Orthodox Church and the Russian government: the illumination of America with the light of the Orthodox faith.

The further fate of New Valaam and its residents is told in Appendix 1.

The Fate of New Valaam
by Lydia Black

By 1877, ten years after the sale of Alaska to the United States of America, New Valaam had become uninhabited. Sof'ia Vlasova died (✝1861 or 1862); Gerasim Zyrianov (✝1869) and Koz'ma Uchilishchev (✝1861) also died. The last to die, as Venerable Herman predicted, was the Aleut Ignatius Alig-iaga (✝1874). Hieromonk Anatoly (Kamenskii, later archbishop of Irkutsk) saw the crosses over their graves in 1896. Others, old and young residents, even earlier moved away from New Valaam, having founded their own village some distance away, in Pestriakovskiaia Bay. But the holy place was not empty for long. Soon a monk from Valaam Monastery, Hieromonk Nikita, took up residence there.

Hieromonk Nikita (Marchenko), a former officer, wanted to go to New Valaam for many years. He arrived

on Kodiak in 1879. He brought with him from Valaam
Monastery an icon of the venerable Saints Sergius and
Herman of Valaam for the chapel of the Meeting of the
Lord on Spruce Island, but it was placed in Holy Res-
urrection Church on Kodiak. This icon remains there to
this day. It is now kept on Spruce Island in the chapel that
was built from 1894 to 1896 over the grave of Venerable
Herman.

Hieromonk Nikita was assigned to the Kodiak church
and served in it until the end of 1880. That year he was
appointed to serve in the Kenai mission, where he labored
until 1885. He never gave up his dream to live on Spruce
Island. He wrote petitions both to the ecclesiastical administration and to the Alaskan bishop requesting permission
to live at New Valaam at the grave of the elder Herman.
Then the ober-procurator of the Most-Holy Synod sent a
telegraph, through the Russian Consulate in Washington,
ordering Hieromonk Nikita to return to Russia.

Despite this order, in 1886 Hieromonk Nikita decided
on this own to move to Spruce Island. He settled in the
same glade where the cell of Venerable Herman had
been and where Sof'ia Vlasova as well as Gerasim Zyrianov and his family had lived after the death of the elder.
He built himself there a small house, a separate cell,
and other structures. He cleaned up the burial places of
Venerable Herman and monk Joseph and placed grave
markers on their graves. Hieromonk Anatoly described
them this way,

I hurried to the grave of Father Herman, which is located further in a thicket of forest. . . . A clearing smaller than the one
that we had passed through, opened up. In this clearing, on the
elevated left side, there were three wooden structures, somewhat dilapidated from old age. To the left of the entrance was
the low grave of Father Joseph made from thick boards; to the
right—another grave, of a larger size, in the form of a small
house with a roof, the kind that can be seen on Valaam Island
near the so-called "desert" and also with a cross at the head.
This is the grave marker of Father Herman that was built by
Father Nikita. An inscription, cut into the wall, states: "Hieromonks Nikita and Vladimir."

The third structure described by Father Anatoly, a
marker within the fence, was probably over the grave of
Sof'ia Vlasova. On Kodiak, oral tradition says that she
was buried at the feet of Venerable Herman and Father
Joseph, who were buried side by side, according to St
Herman's instructions.

It was not Hieromonk Nikita's destiny to found a skete
there. On the night of December 25, 1887, he burned to
death in a fire of unknown origin. The residents of the
village Ouzinkie, who look after New Valaam to this day,
informed the priest of the Kodiak church of what had
happened. A special commission composed of an American doctor and Alexander Petelin, a reader and former
medical assistant at the Russian hospital in Kodiak (later
he became a priest), investigated the site of the fire. In the

corner of the house where the door had been, they found a handful of charred vertebrae and a baked heart. The remains were brought to Kodiak and buried with the rite of burial for a monk on January 1, 1888. In 1896, Hieromonk Anatoly saw "traces of the fire site, which had not yet been overgrown by weeds. . . . They also showed me the place where they found the charred remains. At the fire site, melted rock and other cast-iron things are scattered around to this day. The entire house, made of thick beams, was turned to ash, but to the continued amazement of the surrounding residents—the ancient spruce trees, beneath the shadow of which the burning house stood, remained unharmed." The account of this fire is passed on by word of mouth in the Kodiak region to this day.

In the 1890s (and perhaps even earlier), Riuppe and Moonin returned to New Valaam. The descendants of Moonin still live in Alaska; many years later, one of them was the priest of the Kenai parish. In 1898, Hieromonk Anatoly wrote about them, "Only three of its [New Valaam's] permanent residents remain: the Riuppe couple and Moonin. The zeal and love of these elderly recluses to the place of repose of Herman and the house of God deserves note." Riuppe remained on Spruce Island until the end of his days. In 1904, "the old man Z. [Zakharii] Riuppe, the volunteer guard of the chapel and grave of Herman," already a widower, met Father Shalamov on his regular visit to New Valaam.

In 1894, the year of the 100th anniversary of the establishment of Orthodoxy in America, the diocesan authorities remembered Father Herman and put a monument over his grave. It was white, and as Hieromonk Anatoly wrote, it was built in the shape of small chapel: its top was designed to hold an icon and a lamp, the flame of which was kept lit by the pious Riuppe couple, who went there on Sundays to pray. An icon of the Savior in a silver setting was placed in the monument.

As early as 1892, Bishop Nicholas (Ziorov), after visiting New Valaam, ordered that the Kodiak parish priest, Tikhon Shalamov, take all necessary preparatory measures for opening St Herman's relics. He also decided to build a chapel over the grave of the elder. Father Tikhon Shalamov gave the bishop the plan for the chapel; it was designed for 200 parishioners. Bishop Nicholas donated his own personal money to build the chapel, which stood from 1894 to 1896. Father Tikhon supervised the construction. The chapel of Saints Sergius and Herman of Valaam was consecrated on July 5, 1889, by Father Anatoly (Kamenskii), who was by then an archimandrite. Evidently, the icon of Saints Sergius and Herman of Valaam, which had been brought to America by Hieromonk Nikita, was then placed in this chapel. On the eve of the consecration, Archimandrite Anatoly served a *pannikhida* at the cemetery, near the old dilapidated chapel. On the day of the consecration, after the Divine Liturgy and the service for blessing water with a procession of the cross, a *pannikhida* was served at the graves of Venerable Herman and Father Joseph. Father Anatoly wrote that it was obvious that the gathered multitude was waiting for the opening of the relics of Venerable Herman. The dean of the diocese at that time and the future archpastor and new-martyr Anatoly wrote, "Everyone believes that they are incorrupt."

Despite the fact that the inhabitants of New Valaam gradually moved away during the last decade of the nineteenth century, the majority of them remained on Spruce Island and often visited the place of the ascetic struggles of the elder and cared for his grave. As was mentioned earlier, from time to time someone returned to New Valaam to live permanently. At least once a year, people from all of the Kodiak villages visited the old chapel and the graves of Venerable Herman and his fellow strugglers, as Father Tikhon Shalamov attested in his notes.

Beginning in the 1890s, when Bishop Nicholas visited this holy place, not a single Alaskan bishop has failed to visit New Valaam. On July 28, 1899, not long after his arrival in America, Bishop Tikhon (Belavin), the future confessor and patriarch of all Russia, visited New Valaam. Vladyka Tikhon served a *pannikhida* at the graves of monk Herman, monk Joseph, and Hieromonk Nikita, praying for the peace of their souls. Then St Tikhon examined the contents of the new chapel of Saints Sergius and Herman of Valaam. The kamilavka[212] of St Herman was there; he gave it to Father Shalamov and ordered that in the future it be kept in Holy Resurrection Church on Kodiak. Later, the kamilavka was returned to New Valaam, but after the glorification of Venerable Herman in 1970, it was returned again to Holy Resurrection Church on Kodiak and placed on the shrine of the saint. Also sent to Holy Resurrection Church were old service books, which Vladyka found at the site of the cell of Venerable Herman, where Hieromonk Nikita had built himself a small cell (it did not burn) in addition to a house.

With the death of the old man Riuppe at the start of the twentieth century, New Valaam again became deserted. From time to time, pious laymen who had a particular veneration for St Herman settled there.

Many hierarchs expressed a desire to found a monastery there, but no concrete actions toward this were taken. Even when Archimandrite Gerasim (Schmaltz) settled at New Valaam, a monastery did not grow on that site.

Father Gerasim, a native of Kaluga, became a novice in the St Tikhon Monastery in Kaluga in 1906, before he had even turned eighteen years old. In 1915, he arrived in America, and on April 24, 1915, was tonsured a monk. October 12/25 of the same year, he was ordained a hieromonk. In August 1916, he was sent to Sitka[213] in Alaska, and in November he was assigned the priest of the Afognak parish.

He first visited New Valaam in May 1927. By his own choice, he later lived in the village of Ouzinkie on Spruce

Island. In 1935, he had a vision: Venerable Herman rang the Paschal bells and called him to New Valaam. Father Gerasim, soon thereafter, moved to New Valaam; in 1936, the residents of Ouzinkie built a tiny house for him there. A small chapel was built on the site of Venerable Herman's cell. In that same year, Father Gerasim opened the grave of the holy elder. Local oral tradition says that he washed the bones in a stream, according to the practice of Athonite monks (Father Gerasim spent a year on Mt Athos, in 1911 to 1912). The relics of Venerable Herman were placed in a burial vault, obtained by Father Gerasim and painted by Hieromonk Seraphim. The boards from the coffin remain in the Chapel of the Kaluga Icon of the Mother of God to this day. The kamilavka and iron cross with paraman were also kept there in a glass case. Now they are in Holy Resurrection Church in Kodiak, in the shrine where the relics of the saint are kept. It should be noted that as early as January 21/February 3, 1934, the priest of Holy Resurrection Church in Kodiak, Archpriest Nicholas Kashevarov, had submitted a report to Bishop Alexei with a request to open the elder's grave by the 100th anniversary of his repose, because he was venerated by the local population as a saint. The spiritual authorities were ordered to begin gathering and recording evidence of signs and miracles that had occurred by the intercession of the elder Herman. On March 16, 1934, approval was sent back to the already aged Father Nicholas Kashevarov.

Somewhat later, Bishop Alexei (Panteleev), earnestly raised the question about the glorification of Venerable Herman. By this time, Archimandrite Gerasim had little by little gathered donations for the founding of a monastery on Spruce Island and was being called the treasurer of the future community. Bishop Alexei decided that the monastery would be created and began to gather funds with great energy. Collections for the monastery occurred in Alaska during Great Lent in all Alaskan churches and chapels. When Hierodeacon Il'ia (Shchukin) arrived in Alaska in 1938, Bishop Alexei decided to begin construction. A place was chosen, and at the initiative of the bishop, an application for a 160-acre homestead was submitted to the government. In 2000, a search for records in the archives of the Bureau of Land Management brought no results. Evidently, soon after the application for land in the name of the Hierodeacon Shchukin had been submitted following the proper procedure, it was lost.

At the beginning of May 1939, construction began about two miles from New Valaam on the shore of a small, unnamed lake that was surrounded by dense forest. The builders of the monastery, besides Bishop Alexei and Hierodeacon Il'ia, were fifteen residents of the village of Ouzinkie. The contractor was Nicholas Pestriakov. His sons worked with him along with the Ponomarevs, the Kotel'nikovs, and others. Their descendants still live in Ouzinkie and on Kodiak Island. They care for the deserted New Valaam, Venerable Herman's grave, and

Father Gerasim (Schmaltz's) grave. By the end of the summer, they had built a house for the future brotherhood, but no one answered the call of Bishop Alexei. After a year or two, Hierodeacon Il'ia had to leave Spruce Island. In 1947, he served in the Church of the Protection of the Most-Holy Theotokos on Second Street in New York. This is the same church where to this day there is an icon of St Herman that depicts scenes from his life. Archimandrite Seraphim painted it in 1929; it is one of two icons painted long before the glorification of Venerable Herman [more about the second icon below].

In 1948, at the request of Bishop Ioann (Zlobin), the residents of Ouzinkie, with the aid of rowboats, floated a house from Icon Bay to the bay of New Valaam, which is now called Monk's Lagoon. It was thought that this building would be a guesthouse for pilgrims. From time to time in the 1980s, Hegumen Gerasim (Vurik) lived in this house alone, in prayer, with permission of the diocesan authorities.

According to the St Herman's Brotherhood, the Athonite schema-monk Macarius joined Father Gerasim (Schmaltz) in 1946, but he could not endure the climate and moved to Canada, to Archimandrite Ambrose (Konovalov), the long-time spiritual guide of Father Gerasim.

In 1951, the diocesan authorities temporarily assigned Father Gerasim to the Afognak parish, which at that time had no priest. Heiromonk Sergii (Irtel') was to have substituted for him on Spruce Island. Father Gerasim refused this assignment, thoroughly rejecting Father Sergius' request to build a separate cell on the shore at New Valaam. According to evidence gathered by Hegumen Herman (Podmoshenskii), Father Sergius and his cell attendant (perhaps Hieromonk Seraphim, who later left the spiritual orders of his own free will) first built themselves a cell, as Father Sergius wanted, on the shore of the lagoon, and then they moved to the southern side of Spruce Island, having built a cell or small hermitage. They named this small hermitage for St John the Baptist. Father Sergius slept in one cell in a casket, which still exists. But soon, Father Sergius abandoned Spruce Island. He was assigned to serve in the Klinkit village of Kilisnu. Father Sergius, in the end, left Alaska and lived out the remainder of his days in Mexico, where he accepted the great schema with the name Theodore. It is said that he undertook the ascetic struggle of being a fool-for-Christ. He died in 1996.

Several laymen also resided at New Valaam in this period. Basil Bushkovskii (currently written Boskofskii) built a small house with two tiny rooms. Hieromonk Joseph (Tucker) currently resides in this small house, which is called by the locals "Vasya's home." Hieromonk Joseph stays there from time to time, when the diocesan authorities allow him to temporarily leave his responsibilities in Ouzinkie, Larson's Harbor, and Port Lions—remote settlements on Kodiak Island. His dream is to reside there permanently, having taken the schema.

Currently[214] there are no monastic inhabitants in New Valaam. A monastic community, founded by the St Herman's Brotherhood, exists on Spruce Island. A female community, also founded by the brotherhood, and at one time located on Spruce Island, moved to tiny Nelson's Island, which is separated from Spruce Island by a narrow strait. The history of the founding of the brotherhood and the monastic communities close by New Valaam are set forth below.

In the summer of 1961, reader Gleb Podmoshenskii had just finished seminary at Holy Trinity Monastery in Jordanville, New York; the rector of the seminary was the since-reposed Bishop Averky. Brother Gleb longed to go to Alaska, to visit the holy place where Venerable Herman once struggled. Vladyka blessed Podmoshenskii's plans and supplied him with the following letter:

6/19 July, 1961

Епископ Аверкий

Ректор Свято-Троицкой Духовной Семинарии

Bishop Averky

Rector of the Holy Trinity Orthodox Seminary

Jordanville, New York

The bearer of this, reader Gleb Podmoshenskii, has a bachelor of Theology, having finished this year the full course of the Holy Trinity Orthodox Seminary in Jordanville, New York.

Reader Gleb Podmoshenskii is bound for Alaska to venerate the holy relics of that place's ascetic struggler in piety, the elder HERMAN, and along the way he is undertaking a missionary assignment—to acquaint believers with Holy Trinity Monastery and with Holy Trinity Orthodox Seminary which is located there.

With this letter, I earnestly ask you to extend your utmost assistance and all the help within your power to reader Gleb for the greater success of the good aims he has established.

(signed) +Bishop Averky

Rector of the Holy Trinity Seminary

in Jordanville

Father Gerasim met reader Gleb and spoke with him at length. While reading the books that Father Gerasim supplied him and praying in the Chapel of the Valaam Ascetics Saints Sergius and Herman, Gleb found the goal of his life—to serve the memory of the elder Herman. Both Father Gerasim and, after Gleb's return to Jordanville, Vladyka Averky blessed Gleb to paint an icon of Venerable Herman, although the elder had not yet been glorified by the Church. This icon was placed by St John of Shanghai and San Francisco in the altar of the Chapel of St Tikhon in the orphanage where St John served. Vladyka John also blessed Podmoshenskii to establish St Herman's Brotherhood.

The brotherhood was founded in San Francisco by reader Gleb and his companion, the future Father Seraphim (Eugene Rose) in 1963. When Father Gerasim (Schmaltz) learned of this, he sent the brotherhood their first donation of twenty-five dollars. He also sent the brotherhood an antique brass icon of the Mother of God, which he had found on the shore of the lagoon. Father Gerasim considered that this icon had belonged to Venerable Herman at some point. When the brotherhood founded a monastery in Platina, California, in 1969, this icon along with the icon which brother Gleb had painted in 1962 were brought to the new community. In 1970, brother Gleb was tonsured a monk with the name Herman. Subsequently he became the first hegumen of the monastery of St Herman in Platina. Today he lives in retirement near Platina.

In 1983, seven brothers arrived on Spruce Island and took up residence in the so-called Deacon's House, which had been built in 1939 under the direction of Bishop Alexei of Alaska and moved to New Valaam by the local Aleuts, as was noted earlier. Three of the monks, as it had been in the past, could not endure the solitary life at New Valaam. Only four monks remained there. Unfortunately, Bishop Gregory (Afonskii, of the Orthodox Church of America) did not allow them to live at New Valaam. Then they moved their community to Pleasant Harbor, on the southern side of Spruce Island, where the couple Edward and Anna Opheim sold the brotherhood five acres for a very meager sum. In 1983, the brotherhood built their first building there, which the locals call "the monks' house." This is how the Skete of the Holy Archangel Michael began.

The brotherhood lived in the skete until 1986, when they turned their community over to the nuns. In 1990 or 1991, the nuns, who keep the monastic rule of Valaam Monastery, moved to Nelson's Island, where they founded the Skete of St Nil; they also called their island the Island of St Nil. That year, the monks returned to the Skete of the Archangel Michael, but they didn't abandon the dream to found a community at New Valaam.

In 1993, one member of the brotherhood moved into Vasya's Home, which he repaired. The monks established a very good, close relationship with the Aleuts from Ouzinkie and with the directors of the Ouzinkie Corporation, to which almost all of the territory of the former New Valaam belonged, with the exception of two acres belonging to the Orthodox Church of America. With the verbal agreement of the corporation, the monks from the skete and from the monastery of St Herman began to move to New Valaam in 1994. All together, the brotherhood diligently began the repair of the remaining old buildings and the construction of new ones.

In 1995, with the permission of the corporation, the monks built a new, small chapel dedicated to the Meeting of the Lord. The chapel stands on approximately the same place that a chapel previously stood during the time of St Herman and his successors, almost until the end of the nineteenth century. The interior of the chapel is frescoed with surprising mastery. The icons illustrate the arrival of the first Orthodox mission to Alaska in 1794 and episodes from the life of Venerable Herman. Not far away on the path leading to this chapel, one member of the brotherhood built an entrance gate decorated with a cross.

Five monks settled on New Valaam. On Holy Trinity Day in 1997, the foundation was laid for the main building of the monastery: a tower of several stories (now known as the refectory). Its gilded cupola greets pilgrims from afar; it is visible from the sea while approaching the lagoon by boat.

Meanwhile, the brotherhood grew, so that each monk built himself a secluded, semi-dugout cell throughout the forest of New Valaam. But they did not have long to live in their desired home. The dean of St Herman's Orthodox Seminary on nearby Kodiak Island was concerned that the monks did not belong to the Orthodox Church of America, as at that time their canonical status was called into question by many. He made his opinions known to the Aleuts of Ouzinkie with the result that on May 6, 1998, the director of the native corporation ordered the monks to immediately leave New Valaam. The monks did not protest and returned to the Skete of the Holy Archangel Michael with the support of benevolently inclined laypeople and, especially, the Opheims. Thanks to this couple, the territory of the skete expanded and the community grew. Both the monks and the educational institution for adolescents they founded in the town of Kodiak enjoy great respect among the Kodiak residents of all confessions, including the Orthodox. But the unfinished monastic buildings and cells in New Valaam still stand empty.

APPENDIX 2

The Glorification of the Venerable Herman of Alaska, the Wonder-Worker

Venerable Herman was glorified July 27/August 9, 1970, by the Russian Orthodox Church Outside of Russia in San Francisco and at the same time by the Orthodox Church of America on Kodiak Island. Included here are descriptions of the glorification of Venerable Herman by the Russian Orthodox Church Outside of Russia, written by a participant in the San Francisco ceremony, the well-known émigré iconographer Archimandrite Cyprian (Pizhov) and a participant in the Kodiak ceremony, Lydia Black.[215]

CELEBRATION IN SAN FRANCISCO

Archbishop Anthony and the Brotherhood of St Herman, which now has withdrawn to the mountains of California, prepared for the celebration of the glorification with unusual zeal; the service with the canon was carefully worked out both there and here in the monastery. The holiness, depth, and spiritual essence of this church event was revealed to everyone in full force on the very day of the glorification. At the moment when the moleben for the blessing of water was served in the narthex of the cathedral by Archpriest Il'ia Venem, who was surrounded by a small group of pilgrims, some kind of unexpected, completely new feeling entered inside the heart and did not subside for almost every minute of the liturgy and the rest of the day.

I heard many people say, "It is like Pascha!" And, truly, on the outside it did resemble Pascha: the white vestments of the clergy, the white covers on the analoys, the multitude of candles, and the bright faces of the pilgrims; but Paschal joy belongs to the resurrection of Christ, and this was but a bright reflection—one that was unexpected and remarkable, one which made the length of the six-hour service unnoticeable even for children and feeble old men.

By the start of the vigil on Saturday, the clergy had begun to gather; in two long lines they exited for the "meeting" of Metropolitan Philaret, thirty people in all and five deacons. Besides the local hierarchs, Archbishop Anthony and Bishop Nectarios, Archbishop Vitaly of Montreal and Canada, and Bishop Laurus of Manhattan also attended.

The resurrectional vigil was combined with the service to the newly glorified saint—Venerable Herman of

Alaska the Wonder-Worker. For the first time the sti-
cheras, which were composed for this special service with
inspiration and skillfully performed, were sung during
"Lord, I have cried" and the litya. At the polyeleos, the
metropolitan and the hierarchs serving with him exited
the altar to the singing of "Praise ye the name of the
Lord" by an expanded choir under the direction of M. S.
Konstantinov; then the protopresbyters, archimandrites,
archpriests, hegumens, priests, deacons, subdeacons, and
a multitude of altar servers of various ages followed. Pilgrims holding lit candles surrounded them, filling the
nave to the solea. Lying in the center, on an analoy decorated with flowers, among a plethora of burning candles,
covered with a white shroud, and tied with ribbon—an
icon of Venerable Herman with a particle from his relics
and coffin.

The collective attention of the pilgrims was in the
direction of the analoy. After the last laudatory "alle-
luia," the metropolitan came down from the cathedra
and, having crossed himself broadly with the sign of the
cross, untied the ribbons and removed the shroud. At that
moment, "We glorify thee, O Venerable Father Herman,
and we venerate thy holy memory, instructor of monastics and converser with angels," resounded forth (or if it
is permissible to express it this way—"thundered forth")
from the priests. The repetition of the glorification floated
down from above, as if from the cupola with the depic-
tion of the Lord of Sabaoth, sitting on cherubims and

seraphims. During the alternating singing of the choir and the twenty-four priests, four deacons censed the Venerable One, filling the church with aromatic incense.

There was similarly festal, alternating, harmonized singing of the clergy and the choir for the singing of the resurrectional "The Choir of Angels," and "Blessed art Thou, O Lord." Metropolitan Philaret censed the altar with two archdeacons. The reading of the Gospel, anointing with oil—during which Vladyka Antony gave out printed icons of Venerable Herman—and reading of the canons followed. Brother Gleb Podmoshenskii, one of those who labored on its composition, read the canon to Venerable Herman.

The All-Night Vigil finished at midnight.

The services on Sunday, the next day, were even more impressive, more joyous, and more festal. For the fervor in keeping the memory of this God-pleaser, the Lord generously rewarded us, sinful people, who had filled the church on the day of his glorification; the Grace of the Holy Spirit warmed dry hearts and the six-hour service passed without notice.

God's help to those who were working on the frescoing[216] of the cupola cannot be overlooked: no one supposed that the scaffolding that was all around the inside walls of the church would be dismantled by the day of the glorification. It was dark in the church, thanks to the solid deck of boards placed at the base of the barrel of the cupola—the only source of daylight, since all twenty-four windows are located inside of it, above the boards. It was suggested to decorate the scaffolding with branches and flowers, but by the prayers of Venerable Herman, it was possible to finish the fresco. The scaffolding was removed on Friday before the conciliar serving of the last service for the departed for the ever-memorable monk, elder Herman. But after this it immediately became radiant—everyone was glad that the scaffolding had been removed, that the cupola was frescoed, and that it was possible to pray in the bright church under a canopy depicting overhead the Lord of Sabaoth, blessing those present and praying.

At the end of the liturgy, Metropolitan Philaret gave an inspired sermon, in which he glorified God and Venerable Herman as a newfound Russian God-pleaser, who has now been entered in the list of saints of the Russian Church.

After a moleben with a procession of the cross, during which the icon of Venerable Herman was lifted high, and the singing of "Many Years," Archbishop Anthony greeted Metropolitan Philaret, who had led this magnificent celebration, the visiting hierarchs, priests, choir, and all pilgrims who had made the effort to attend.

A special synodal honor was awarded to the brothers in Christ—Eugene, Gleb, and Lawrence, for having particularly labored in the gathering of material for the glorification of Venerable Herman.

Archbishop Vitaly served the evening service in honor of the Smolensk Icon of the Mother of God.

On Monday, Archbishop Antony led the hierarchical liturgy.

This is how the unforgettable days of the glorification of the newfound Russian God-pleaser, Venerable Herman of Alaska the Wonder-Worker, were concluded.

It is also necessary to note, that all of these days lacked the San Francisco fog—a summer sun shone and gave warmth like in the south. The Orthodox exclaimed and rejoiced. Wednesday, after the conclusion of the celebrations, the gray fog returned and hung over the streets of San Francisco. Everything took on the typical, weekday appearance—neither warm, nor cold.

O! If only this "neither-warm-nor-cold" feeling would disappear from our hearts sometime, like it did on the foggy streets of San Francisco!

CELEBRATION ON KODIAK ISLAND
By Lydia Black

An assembly of hierarchs of the Orthodox Church of America, headed by Metropolitan Ireney, set sail for New Valaam, where the coffin with the relics of the elder that had been found by Father Gerasim (Schmaltz) had been opened. They were placed in a new coffin that had been made of various kinds of Alaskan wood by the Anchorage resident D. H. Keathley in 1969. The wood, including spruce from Spruce Island and aromatic Alaskan cedar, was blessed in the Cathedral of St Innocent of Irkutsk in Anchorage. Keathley, who was named Herman when he accepted Orthodoxy, carved traditional Russian and Greek Orthodox crosses on the burial vault.

The relics were transferred to Kodiak by helicopter and placed in the altar of Holy Resurrection Church. On Sunday, August 8 (n.s.) at 7:00 p.m., the act of canonization was read. After the reading, the All-Night Vigil was served. The service was conducted in English. Metropolitan Ireney, Archbishop Paul of Finland, Metropolitan Andrew of Bulgaria, Archbishop John of Chicago, Archbishop Cyprian of Philadelphia, Bishop Theodosius of Sitka, Bishop Joseph of Edmonton, and Bishop Dmitry of Berkeley (California) all participated in the service. For the first time, the words of a prayer to Venerable Herman were heard in a church. A new icon of Venerable Herman was blessed during the service. This icon is now located in Holy Resurrection Church in Kodiak.

After the end of the All-Night Vigil, the church remained opened, and many prayed at his shrine all night. Early in the morning, an early liturgy was led by Bishops Theodosius, Joseph, and Dmitry. Fifteen priests served with them. At 10:00 p.m., a late liturgy was served, in which Metropolitan Ireney, Archbishop Paul of Finland, Metropolitan Andrew of Bulgaria, Archbishop John of Chicago, and Archbiship Cyprian of Philadelphia participated. Twenty-five priests served with them. An Aleut choir, having come from all ends of the Alaskan territory and the Pribilov Islands, sang part of the service in Aleut. Part of the singing in Aleut had been written by Bishop Alexei (Panteleev). The church was overflowing for both services, so that many prayed outside. There were two processions with the cross: during a special moleben and after liturgy on Sunday. After the procession with the cross, Bishop Theodosius lowered the coffin into the shrine, which had been special ordered from a craftsman in New York. After the service, many went to New Valaam, where a moleben to St Herman was served.

The festivities attracted many guests, including the governor of the state of Alaska, Keith Miller. Before the celebration of the glorification, on August 4, 1970, Senator Ted Stevens entered his speech about Venerable Herman and a brief biography of him in the *Congressional Record.*[217]

The shrine with the relics of Venerable Herman is located in Holy Resurrection Church in Kodiak. On its lid in the center Venerable Herman is depicted and on the sides are Archangels Michael and Gabriel. The chains, cross, and kamilavka of St Herman lie on top of the shrine. Every Thursday at 6:30 p.m., an akathist is served to the saint. Some of the parishioners never miss this service, which ends with a kneeling prayer to the holy elder. Many local residents turn to him without ceremony, calling him "*Appa*"—grandfather; they often come to the shrine with his relics with their requests and prayers.

Every year, starting in 1970, believers come together from the ends of the earth to participate in the yearly pilgrimage to Spruce Island on the day of the glorification of the elder Herman. As the Kodiak priest Basil Martish wrote back in 1906 about a pilgrimage taken to New Valaam by Bishop Innocent (Pustinskii) in 1905, "I do not know, if anywhere else on earth there is such a fitting place for self-introspection and the struggle of prayer than on Spruce Island. Here the insufferable sounds of daily life are not heard: peace and quiet reign all around, and nothing distracts from the atmosphere of prayer. Here it is easy to pray!"

Eyewitnesses

Baranov, Alexander Andreevich (1749–1819) Baranov was hired by Grigorii Shelikhov in 1790 as administrator of the company on Kodiak Island. He was subordinate only to Shelikhov but had to follow Russian laws and execute governmental decrees. He set out for Alaska on the ship *Three Hierarchs* in the fall of 1790. The vessel, under the command of Dmitry Bocharov, was broken up by a strong gale in Koshigen Harbor on Unalaska Island. Baranov wintered on Unalaska. In the spring of 1791, he departed for Kodiak in a *baidarka*. He arrived in Three Saints Harbor on June 27, 1791. In 1792, he founded Pavlovskaia Harbor in Chiniatsk Bay (the modern city of Kodiak) and moved the center of the company's operations there. He was removed from his post through governmental decrees by Captain Golovnin and Captain Hagemeister in 1818. He died on the ship *Kutuzov* on April 16, 1819. His body was buried at sea, in Sunda Strait. Baranov was married but had no children. They had adopted children, who are usually called the children of Baranov and his first wife, Matrona. On Kodiak, Baranov started a new family, with Anna Grigor'evna Razkazchikov, an Aleut from the village Karluk. They had three children: a son Antipater, who died in St Petersburg; a daughter Irina, who married Lieutenant Simeon Ivanovich Ianovskii; and a daughter Catherine, who married Grigorii Sungurov in Sitka in 1821 and moved with him to Russia in 1825.

Baranov was not well disposed toward the mission, although he made donations for the construction of the church and school. Despite this, at the end of his stay in Alaska relations with the clergy had been sorted out.

After Baranov's departure for Russia, Anna Grigor'evna found refuge with Venerable Herman on Spruce Island. She married a second time to an Aleut in 1821 with the blessing of the elder. In 1836, she returned to Spruce Island and lived by herself with the elder Herman.

Gideon, Hieromonk (circa 1770–1843) In the world, Hieromonk Gideon was known as Gabriel Fedotov and was the son of a priest. He arrived on Kodiak in June 1804 on the *Neva* (commander, Iurii Lisianskii). He left Kodiak in May 1807 and returned to St Petersburg in 1809, after an inspection of the churches in Kamchatka. Near the end of his life, he stayed in Konevsky Monastery. He died in 1843 in St Nikolevskaya Andreevskaya Monastery, Olenets Diocese.[218]

Golovnin, Basil Michaelovich (1776–1831) A naval officer, Golovnin was subsequently naval minister. His first visit to Alaska and Kodiak was in 1810, as commander of the sloop *Diana*. It is not known whether Golovnin met with Venerable Herman on this visit. To all appearances, on his first voyage, such a meeting did not take place.

Golovnin was in Alaska the second time in 1818, commanding the ship *Kamchatka*. Golovnin had broad powers: to clarify the situation in Alaska and to conduct an audit of the Russian-American Company. At his order, Baranov was removed as chief manager and sent to Russia. Some of the documents about the relations between Golovnin and Venerable Herman are kept in the archives of the Russian Navy; other documents are thought to be in the personal archives of Golovnin.

Golovnin held a very high opinion of Venerable Herman. In his essay about his trip around the world on *Kamchatka*, he writes under the date July 10, "In order to better ascertain the real condition of affairs here, I addressed by letter the head of the religious mission here, monk Herman—an intelligent and pious man, it is said, and one whom the greater part of the residents here cannot praise sufficiently."[219]

From this it can be concluded that Golovnin met with Venerable Herman only after July 1818. Golovnin was the very same captain who invited St Herman onto his ship, where the elder led a discussion in the wardroom with his officers (among whom was Wrangell, then a young midshipman, and Murav'ev, then still only a lieutenant).[220] In his report to the Naval Ministry,[221] Golovnin writes (and later, repeating his words, Wrangell says the same thing) that all the clergy on Kodiak were depraved, drunkards, and so on—without any basis or evidence, but makes the comment that "of all of them only monk Herman is a man who is sober, devout, modest, and—in a word—a genuine and true monk, who conducted himself the same all the time; for this, the *promyshlenniki* made attempts on his life several times."[222]

Golovnin goes on to recount:[223]

In order to achieve this goal, after my arrival on Kodiak Island, where the most abused group is, I addressed in writing the head of the local religious mission, the monk Herman, an old man, devout, modest, and sober, about whom all our officers who have been in that region express the highest praise. I insisted on a formal and impartial letter of advice from him, as befits his calling and obligation to God, as to the truth of Mr Lisianskii's and all the travelers' testimony which had been published, regarding the cruelty of the company workers' treatment of the local residents. And he affirmed all of the points of Mr Lisianskii's remarks, that they are completely true and in his own letter, enclosed here under No 3, he also confirmed them.

Hagemeister, Ludwig von (Leontii Andrianovich) (1780–1833) Hagemeister was captain of the ship *Neva* from 1806 to 1810. He wintered on Kodiak 1807–1808 and 1809–1810, and visited Kodiak a second time from March 1810 to April 12, 1810. He returned to Alaska November 21, 1817 as commander of the ship *Kutuzov*. Under the direction of V. M. Golovnin, he conducted the replacement of Baranov and in January 1818 became the chief manager of the Russian colony in America. He left this post because of illness in July 1818. It is not known when he met Venerable Herman, but it is known that in January 1818 he asked (through the manager of the Kodiak office, Gerasim Potorochin) the opinion and advice of Venerable Herman about a plan to send an expedition to northern Alaska.[224]

Ianovskii, Simeon Ivanovich (1789–1876) A naval officer, Ianovskii began to work for the Russian-American Company (RAC) in 1816. He arrived in America in 1817 on the ship *Suvorov,* on which Lieutenant Ianovskii was the first mate of Captain Ponafidin to Sitka. In Sitka (New Arkhangel'sk), he married Baranov's daughter, Irina Alexandrevna, in January 1818 in the Church of the Archangel Michael. After Baranov's replacement, his younger daughter, Catherine, moved in with them; she was then twelve years old. The Ianovskiis had two children, Alexander and Maria. Both were born in Alaska. Alexander, a naval officer, ended his life as a monk (Hieromonk

Christopher). In Alaska, Ianovskii was the assistant and deputy to Hagemeister. After the departure of Hagemeister, Ianovskii became the chief manager of the Russian colony (1818–1820).

When he accepted the post, he immediately wrote Father Herman about his desire to visit him in Kodiak. A copy of the letter is preserved in the archives of the RAC. Ianovskii was in Kodiak during the flu epidemic of 1819, when Venerable Herman, having left his cell, cared for the sick. After the epidemic, the holy elder took in orphans at his skete and raised them.[225]

Ianovskii left Alaska in 1821. After Irina's death, Ianovskii married a second time, in 1826. From this marriage, there were four children. In 1864, he left his second wife and entered a monastery in Kaluga, taking the schema. He died January 6, 1876. In his letters to Valaam from the 1860s, he called Venerable Herman his spiritual guide. In his memoirs, sent to Valaam in 1864–1865,[226] Ianovskii provides much valuable material, but there are mistakes, particularly in dates. The drawings, which Ianovskii sent to the abbot of the Valaam Monastery, are thought to be the work of his daughter, a nun. This question, about the authorship of these drawings, has not been researched.

Kupreianov, Ivan Antonovich (1799?–1857) Kupreianov was a naval officer, and later, a rear admiral. He was the chief manager of the Russian colonies from 1835 to 1840. He treated the holy elder Herman very well, passing on the icons and books that St Herman had ordered. In 1836, at the elder's request, he appointed Riuppe to help him. It appears that he met with Venerable Herman only once. In 1836, an epidemic of smallpox came to Kodiak, and all of Kupreianov's efforts over the course of two years were directed against it. Two of Kupreianov's letters to Venerable Herman are preserved (see the archives of the Russian-American Company in the National Archives in Washington, D.C.). Kupreianov's report about the death of the elder that was sent to the main office of the RAC in St Petersburg is also preserved.

Murav'ev, Matvei Ivanovich (1784–1836) A naval officer, Murav'ev was the chief manager of the Russian colonies in America from 1820 to 1825. He first met St Herman on Kodiak early in the summer of 1818, when he served on the sloop *Kamchatka* under the command of Golovnin. As his letters to the elder attest, Venerable Herman made an enormous impression on him. These letters are preserved in the archives of the Russian-American Company in the National Archives in Washington, D.C. When the recently arrived, married priest Frumentii Mordovskii tried to submit the remaining members of the mission, Father Herman and Father Athanasius, to his authority (and making a search of their quarters and ordering Venerable Herman to leave Spruce Island), Murav'ev immediately defended them and sent a report through the proper channels to the synod about the illegal actions of Mordovskii.

Wrangell, Ferdinand Peterovich (1796–1870) Wrangell first arrived in Alaska in 1817–1818, as midshipman on the ship *Kamchatka*, under the command of Golovnin. It can be assumed that that was when he first met Venerable Herman. Wrangell was in Alaska a second time in the fall of 1826 as commander of the ship *Krotkii*. It is not known whether he visited Kodiak in the summer of 1826. *Krotkii* left for Kronstadt from Sitka on October 12.

Wrangell served as the chief manager of the Russian colonies in America from 1830 to 1835. He visited Kodiak several times. He was close to St Herman. He sent Father Frumentii Mordovskii out of the colonies, since he had treated the members of the mission very poorly. Mordovskii sent Hieromonk Athanasius to Russia and searched the cell of Venerable Herman, trying to take the money that the holy elder has gathered to build a church. Wrangell transferred Father Sokolov from Sitka to Kodiak. Sokolov was the priest in Kodiak at the time of the death of the saint; he registered the date of his death in the registry books.

Wrangell visited St Herman on Spruce Island in 1831. By his order, the skete on Spruce Island was then officially called, as the elder wished, New Valaam.

Wrangell ordered the construction of a new chapel of the Meeting of the Lord on Spruce Island, in place of the decrepit one, which had been built earlier by Venerable Herman. (Later, in 1857, the Russian-American Company (RAC) again erected a new chapel on the same site.

Now, a wonderful little chapel stands there that was built and frescoed through the efforts of the members of the St Herman's Brotherhood.)

At Wrangell's order, no Aleuts, Creoles, or Russians had the right to settle on the territory of New Valaam without the permission of Father Herman. None of those who lived in New Valaam could be taken to work for the company without his agreement. If any of the residents of New Valaam wanted to enter the service of the company voluntarily, they had to consult with Father Herman. If Father Herman would need to replenish his cattle or get new tools, then he must immediately be given help, without any delays. These facts are contained in a letter of January 13, 1835, from the RAC headquarters to the Russian Department of Manufacture and Internal Trade. This was the answer to an inquiry of the department, directed to the RAC at the request of the ober-procurator of the synod. The synod requested information about the fate of Venerable Herman; the RAC had not informed the synod of anything.[227] Besides this, Wrangell wrote (in another source) that Father Herman asked to send him a new Gospel and that he fulfilled this request.

NOTES

1. Zhizn', *Valaamskago monakha Germana, amerikanskago missionera*. Available in translation, along with other material, in *Little Russian Philokalia, Vol. III: St Herman* (Platina, Calif.: St Herman Press, 1988). Unless noted, other works mentioned exist only in Russian. Russian words have been transliterated according to the Library of Congress system, except in those instances in which an alternative spelling is in general use in English.

2. *Valaamskie Podvizhniki.*

3. *Ocherki po istorii Amerikanskoi pravoslavnoi dukhovnoi missii (Kad'iakskoi missii 1794–1837)* [Studies in the history of the American Orthodox spiritual mission (Kodiak Mission 1794–1837)] (Valaam Monastery, 1894).

4. *Valaamskie missioneri v Amerike (v kontse XVIII stoletiia).*

5. In most instances, names have been rendered in their recognizable English form. Otherwise Russian names are transliterated according to the American Library Association–Library of Congress Romanization tables.

6. The word translated throughout as *province* is *guberniya,* an administrative subdivision of the Russian Empire, akin to a Canadian province or a U.S. state. Like these, their size could vary considerably.

7. F. P. Wrangell, "*Kad'iakskii otdel, ostrov Kad'iak*" [The Kodiak Department, Kodiak Island], in *Russkaia Amerika v neopublikovannykh zapiskakh K.T. Khlebnikova* [Russian America in the unpublished letters of K. T. Khlebnikov,] ed. Roza G. Liapunova and S. G. Fedorova (Leningrad, 1979), 244.

8. Ibid.

9. Although Valaam is an ancient monastery— some sources cite it as having been founded in the tenth century—it was destroyed by Swedish attacks in the seventeenth century. Abbot Nazarius was instrumental in reestablishing the monastic community at Valaam in the late eighteenth century.— Trans.

10. A. Prisadskii, *Kistorii Pravoslavnoi Tserkvu v Amerike: Iubileinyi sbornik. 200-letie otkrytiia Aliaski: 1741–1941* (San Francisco, 1941), 77.

11. *Valaamskii monastyr i ego podvizhniki* [Valaam Monastery and its ascetics] (St Petersburg, 1889), 260.

12. Ibid.

13. *Obshchectvo religiozno-nravstvennogo prosveshcheniia Pravoslavnoi Tserkvi.*

14. *Amerikanskii Pravoslavnii Vestnik* [American Orthodox Messenger].

15. See the Introduction for a detailed discussion of this evidence. Egor is a common Russian variation of the name *Georgii*, or George.—Trans.

16. N. Subbotin, *Arkhimandrit Feofan nastoiatel' Kyrillova-Novoezerskogo monastyria* (St Petersburg, 1862), 69.

17. His title in Russian is *stroitel',* which literally means "builder." This was the title given to hieromonks who were in charge of very small monastic communities. Because such subtleties do not exist in English ecclesiastic terminology, *stroitel'* has been translated in this passage as "superior."—Trans.

18. TsGIA. F. 19. Op. 1. D. No. 11451. L. 1-10b.

19. *German.*—Trans.

20. RGIA. F. 796. On. 63. D. 407. L. 5.

21. N. Ia. Ozertskovskoi, *Puteshestvie po ozeram Ladozhskomu i Onezhskomu* (Peterozavodsk, 1989), 67–69.

22. Serbodol' is now known as Sortavala.

23. *Zhizn' Valaamskago monakha Germana, amerikanskago missionera* [The life of the Valaam monk Herman, an American missionary] (St Petersburg, 1894), 5.

24. *Valaamskii monastyr.*

25. *Valaamskii monastyr,* 263.

26. Precisely on the site of his forest cell, a splendid stone chapel was erected. It was built in Russo-Byzantine style, with multicolored glass in the windows. It was dedicated to the Holy, Equal-to-the-Apostles Saints Constantine and Helen. The chapel was consecrated in 1908 and built with the funds of a Russian officer, who left his military career, became a monk in Valaam, and kept the memory of St Herman with particular reverence. Out of love to the ascetic, he even physically labored to erect this chapel. This same monk, priest-monk Konstantin, was later elevated to the rank of a bishop sometime between 1925 and 1928. —Ed.

27. Wrangell, "*Kad'iakskii otdel, ostrov Kad'iak,*" 246.

28. Bering was a Danish-born sailor who entered the service of the Russian navy in 1704 during the early days of its development under Peter the Great.—Ed.

29. This company later developed into the Russian-American Company (RAC).—Trans.

30. A. V. Zorin, "'*Pervyi fundator': Rossiisko-amerikanskoi kompanii: Shtrikhi k portretu I.L. Golikova.*" *Amerikanskii ezhegodnik 2002* (Moscow, 2004), 170.

31. Archimandrite Macarius, *Skazanie o zhizni i trudakh preosviashchenneishego Gabriela, mitropolita Novgorodskogo I Sankt-Peterburgskogo* [Stories of the life and labors of his grace Gabriel, metropolitan of Novgorod and St Petersburg] (St Petersburg, 1857), 86–87.

32. Ibid., 87–88.

33. A hieromonk is a monk ordained as a priest; a hierodeacon, a monk ordained as a deacon.—Trans.

34. *Ocherk zhizni I apostol'skikh trudov Innokentiia mitropolita Moskovskogo* [Summary of the life and ascetic labors of the metropolitan of Moscow] (New York, 1990), 148.

35. G. I. Shelikhov, "Letter to the director of the Northeastern American Company A. A. Baranov, August 9, 1794," in *Russkie otkrytiia v Tikhom okeane i Severnoi Amerike v XVIII veke* [Russian discoveries in the Pacific Ocean and Northern America in the eighteenth century], ed. A. I. Andreev (Moscow, 1948), 342.

36. S. Okun', *Rossiisko-Amerikanskaia kompaniia* [The Russian-American Company] (Leningrad, 1939), 342.

37. *Russkie otkrytiia v Tikhom okeane,* 345.

38. Ibid., 346.

39. Materials on the history of Valaam monastery. *Archives of the Finnish New Valaam Monastery* (Leningrad), 81–82.

40. Although the name of the ship is literally *The Three Hierarchs* [*Tri Sviatitelia*], in Alaska it is popularly known as *The Three Saints*; the bay on Kodiak Island where this ship put in and on which the first permanent settlement was established is called Three Saints Bay.—Trans.

41. The Russian word *promyshlennik* means "entrepreneur," although the term most frequently

described fur trappers in Siberia and, later, in Alaska. It initially applied to the members of independent fur procurement crews, who were hired by merchants to catch primarily fur seals and sea otters, as well as red, silver, and black foxes, to harvest the fur. Eventually, the word was applied to all Golikov–Shelikhov employees, both Russian and native, as well as Baranov's soldiers.—Trans.

42. The Pomory were independent peasants who settled Russia's White Sea and Arctic Ocean coasts; they excelled in fishing and marine mammal hunting and, after mixing with local populations, developed a distinct culture, lifestyle, and dialect.—Trans.

43. Okun', *Rossiisko-Amerikanskaia kompaniia,* 167.

44. A sticharion is a long-sleeved, full-body liturgical garment worn by all clergy and others serving in the altar during Orthodox divine services.

45. V. Passek, *Ocherki Rossii, kniga 5* [Sketches of Russia, Book 5] (Moscow, 1842), 228.

46. S. Poberevskii, "*Ocherk istorii Pravoslaviia v Amerike* (1794–1867 gg.)" [A sketch of the history of Orthodoxy in America (1784–1867)], in *Pravoslavnaia zhizn'* [Orthodox life], 4 (1994), 26.

47. A *baidarka* is a kayak.—Trans.

48. A. A. Baranov.

49. Poberevskii, "*Ocherk istorii Pravoslaviia v Amerike,*" 26–27.

50. N. N. Bolkhovitinov, "*U istokov Pravoslaviia v Severnoi Amerike (seredina XVIIIv.–1794 god)*" [From

the source of Orthodoxy in North America (mid-18th century to 1794], in *Amerikanskii ezhegodnik* [American annual] (Moscow, 1994), 127.

51. Tlingits are a once-militant tribe of Indians who still live along the southwestern shore of Alaska. In Russian America, *Creole*s were defined as the children of Russians and local natives; they made up a special class, membership in which was inherited though the father's line. Creoles were later equated with the lower middle class.—Ed.

52. The modern city of Kodiak developed from this settlement.

53. Archimandrite Joseph's letter of May 18, 1795 to Shelikhov from Kodiak. Yudin Collection, Box 1, Folder 1, Library of Congress, Manuscript Division. Also in P. A. Tikhmenev, *Istoricheskoe obozrenie obrazovaniia Rossiisko-Amerikanskoi kompanii* [A historical survey of the formation of the Russian-American Company] (St Petersburg, 1863), vol. 2, appendix, 102–3.

54. A. Timov, *Pis'mo Josepha, preosviashchennogo Kad'iakskogo, k rektoru Iaroslavskoi seminarii Ieronimu Poniatskomu* [A letter of Joseph, bishop of Kodiak, to the rector of the Yaroslav Seminary, Ieronim Poniatskii], in *Dushepoleznoe chtenie* [Reading which is good for the soul] 2 (1910): 10.

55. This is how the report was headed in the American publication, although it was sent to Metropolitan Gabriel.

56. *Vladyka* is the Russian form of address for a bishop; the English equivalent is *master.*—Trans.

57. One verst is 3,500 feet or 0.6628 miles; 300 versts is 198 miles.

58. "A report from Archimandrite Joseph to his archbishop concerning conditions in the Russian settlement on Kodiak Island, in Russian penetration of the North Pacific Ocean 1700–1797," in *To Siberia and Russian America*, ed. B. Dmytryshyn, E. A. P. Crowhart-Vaughan, and T. Vaughan (Portland, Ore.: Historical Society Press, 1988), 2: 476–78.

59. Archimandrite Joseph's letter of May 18, 1795; also in *Istoricheskoe obozrenie obrazovaniia,* 101–7.

60. The accepted spelling in English is *Kodiak.*—Trans.

61. Pasek, *Ocherki Rossii* [Sketches of Russia], 224–28.

62. Ivan III, the Great, ruled Muscovite Russia from 1462 to 1505; during his reign, Moscow conquered Novgorod, a prosperous commercial center.—Trans.

63. In Siberia, a *kocha* is a large, decked river craft with oars and sails.—Trans.

64. This refers to Father Theophan, with whom St Herman became close during his stay in Sarov Monastery from 1773 to 1777 and also to Father Joachim from Sarov Monastery, who had refused to travel to America.

65. 180 pounds.—Trans.

66. 54 pounds.—Trans.

67. Pasek, *Ocherki Rossii* [Sketches of Russia], 230–34; also in Hieromonk Gideon, *The Round the World Voyage of Hieromonk Gideon, 1803–1809*, translated with introduction, notes and additional materials by Lydia Black, ed. Richard A. Pierce (Kingston, Ontario: Limestone Press, 1989).

68. Poberevskii, *Ocherk istorii Pravoslaviia v Amerike,* 18–19.

69. I. E. Veniaminov, "*Sostoianie Pravoslavnoi Tserkvi v rossiiskoi Amerike*" [The state of the Orthodox Church in Russian America], in *Tvoreniia Innokentiia, mitropolita Moskovskogo* [The works of Innocent, metropolitan of Moscow], collected by Ivan Barsukov (Moscow, 1887), 2: 6.

70. I. E. Veniaminov, *Zapiski ob ostrovakh Unalashkinskogo otdela* [Notes on the islands of the Unalaska District] (St Petersburg, 1840), 2: 145; this work has been translated by Lydia T. Black and R. H. Geoghegan (Kingston, Ontario: Limestone Press, 1984).

71. An artel is cooperative organization whose members typically elect one of their own to lead their organization.—Trans.

72. A *toion* is a leader of a village.—Trans.

73. "A report of Hieromonk Macarius," from *Russian penetration of the North Pacific Ocean 1700–1797,* vol. 2, *To Siberia and Russian America*, ed. B. Dmytryshyn, E. A. P. Crowhart-Vaughan, and

T. Vaughan (Portland: Oregon Historical Society Press, 1988), 497–502.

74. *Pis'mo o. Gideona mitropolity Amvrosiiu ot 1 iiunia 1805 g.* [A letter of Father Gideon to Metropolitan Ambrose of June 1, 1805], in *Russkaia Amerika: Po lichnim vpechatlenniiam missionerov, zemleprokhodtsev, moriakov, issledovatelei I drugikh ochevidtsev* [Russian America: By the personal impressions of missionaries, travelers, sailors, investigators and other witnesses], ed. A. D. Drudzo and R. V. Kizhalov (Moscow, 1994), 87.

75. A. N. L'vov, "*Kratkie istorisheskie svedeniia ob uchrezhdenii v Severnoi Amerike pravoslavnoi missii, ob osnovanii Kad'iakskoi eparkhii I deiatel'nosti tam pervykh missionerov*" [Brief historical information about the establishment in North America of an Orthodox mission, about the founding of the Kodiak diocese and the activities of the first missionaries there], in *Tserkovye Vedomosti* [Church News], 39 (1894): 1364.

76. P. I. Pezhemskii and V. A. Krotoc, *Irkutskaia letonis'* [Irkutsk chronicle] (Irkutsk, 1911), 155.

77. A sazhen is an old Russian measure of length equal to seven feet.—Trans.

78. The roots of daylilies are tubers that resemble potatoes and are a staple in the diet.—Trans.

79. *Zapiski ieromonakha Gideona o Pervom russkom krugosvetnom puteshectbii I Russkoi Amerike* [Notes of Hieromonk Gideon about the first Russian around-the-world trip and Russian America], in *Russkaia Amerika:*

Po lichnim vpechatlenniiam missionerov [Russian America: By the personal impressions of missionaries], 84–86.

80. Baron Ferdinand Wrangell served as colonial chief manager of the RAC from 1830 to 1835—Trans.

81. Wrangell, *"Kad'iakskii otdel, ostrov Kad'iak,"* 244.

82. *Pis'mo Baranova k Larionovu ot 24 iiulia 1800 goda* [A letter of Baranov to Larionov from 24 July 1800] in Tikmenev, *Istoricheskoe obozrenie obrazovaniia* [A historical survey of the formation], Vol. 2, appendix, 158–59.

83. The *eikonom* of a monastery is responsible for all purchases of food, clothes, and other essentials.—Tran.

84. A *baidarka* is an open, oar-propelled skin boat similar to a kayak.—Trans.

85. *Pis'mo o. Gideona mitropolity Amvrosiiu ot 2 iiunia 1805 g.* [A letter of Father Gideon to Metropolitan Ambrose from June 2, 1805], in *Russkaia Amerika: Po lichnim vpechatlenniiam missionerov* [Russian America: By the personal impressions of missionaries], 89–91.

86. This is a reference to Tsar Peter the Great, who in 1721 issued the Spiritual Regulation, a set of regulations governing the Russian Orthodox Church that, in many ways, submitted the Church to the state, most notably by replacing the Patriarch with the Most-Holy Synod.—Tran.

87. *Pis'mo A.A. Baranova k Larionovu ot 22 marta 1801 g.* [A letter of A. A. Baranov to Larionov from 22 March 1801] in Tikmenev, *Istoricheskoe obozrenie*

obrazovaniia [A historical survey of the formation], Vol. 2, appendix, 163.

88. Bartolome de las Casas (†1566) was a Spanish monk who defended the rights of native Americans.

89. *Istoriia Russkoi Ameriki (1732–1867), T. 2. Deiatel'nost' Rossiisko-amerikanskoi kompanii (1799–1825)* [History of Russian America (1732–1867), Vol. 2, *Activity of the Russian American Company* (1799–1825)], general ed., N. N. Bolkhovitinov (Moscow, 1999), 48.

90. Easter is called *Pascha* among Orthodox Christians.—Trans.

91. *Pis'mo o. Gideona mitropolity Amvrosiiu ot 2 iiunia 1805 g.* [A letter of Father Gideon to Metropolitan Ambrose from June 2, 1805], in *Russkaia Amerika: Po lichnim vpechatlenniiam missionerov* [Russian America: By the personal impressions of missionaries], 91.

92. Ibid.

93. *Istoriia Russkoi Ameriki (1732–1867), T. 2* [History of Russian America (1732–1867), Vol. 2], 48.

94. L'vov, *Kratkie istorisheskie svedeniia* [Brief historical information about], 1369.

95. Okun', *Rossiisko-Amerikanskaia kompaniia,* 198.

96. Tenerife is one of the Canary Islands, which are located off the coast of Northwest Africa.—Trans.

97. *Pis'mo o. Gideona mitropolity Amvrosiiu; Data ne oboznachena* [A letter of Father Gideon to Metropolitan Ambrose; no date indicated], in *Russkaia Amerika: Po lichnim vpechatlenniiam missionerov*

[Russian America: By the personal impressions of missionaries], 93.

98. *Instruktsiia N. P. Rezanova o. Gideonu ot 25 dekabria 1805 g.* [Instructions of N. P. Rezanov to Father Gideon from December 25, 1805], in *Russkaia Amerika: Po lichnim vpechatlenniiam missionerov* [Russian America: By the personal impressions of missionaries], 44–47.

99. A *bania* is a traditional Russian steam sauna.

100. *Pis'mo o. Gideona mitropolity Amvrosiiu ot 2 iiunia 1805 g.* [A letter of Father Gideon to Metropolitan Ambrose from June 2, 1805], in *Russkaia Amerika: Po lichnim vpechatlenniiam missionerov* [Russian America: By the personal impressions of missionaries], 92.

101. *Izvlechenie is zapisok Langsdorfa, 1803–1807 gg.* [Excerpts from the notes of Langsdorf, 1803–1807], in *Materiali dlia istorii russkikh zaselenii po beregam Vostochnogo okeana* [Materials for the history of the Russian settlements along the coasts of the eastern ocean], 4th ed. (St Petersburg, 1861), 187.

102. Ibid, 191–92.

103. *Dvukratnoe putoshestvie v Ameriku morskikh ofitserov Khvostova and Davydova, pisannoe sim poslednim* [The twofold voyage to America of the naval officers Khvostov and David, written by the latter] (St Petersburg, 1812), 2: 88–90.

104. L'vov, *Kratkie istorisheskie svedeniiu* [Brief historical information about], 1369.

105. V. Peterov, *Kolumbi Rossiiskie* (Washington, 1971), 30.

106. Ivan Kad'iakskii is often mentioned as Ivan Kulikalov. He was the illegitimate son of the RAC employee Demid Il'ich Kulikalov and a Kodiak Aleut.

107. *Izvlechenie is zapisok Langsdorfa* [Excerpts from the notes of Langsdorf], in *Materiali dlia istorii* [Materials for the history], (St. Petersburg, 1861), Fourth Edition, 184–85.

108. *Pis'mo o. Gideona A. A. Baranovu ot 17 maia 1807 g.* [A letter of Father Gideon to A. A. Baranov from May 17, 1807], in *Russkaia Amerika: Po lichnim vpechatlenniiam missionerov* [Russian America: By the personal impressions of missionaries], 103.

109. *Pis'mo o. Gideona k o. Germanu ot 11 iiunia 1807 g.* [A letter of Father Gideon to Father Herman from June 11, 1807], in *Russkaia Amerika: Po lichnim vpechatlenniiam missionerov* [Russian America: By the personal impressions of missionaries], 109–10.

110. *Amerikanskii Pravoslavnii Vestnik* [American Orthodox Messenger], 17 (1899): 469.

111. L'vov, *Kratkie istorisheskie svedeniia* [Brief historical information about], 1369.

112. Wrangell, "*Kad'iakskii otdel*" [The Kodiak Department], in *Russkaia Amerika* [Russian America], 244.

113. More widely known as *Holy Week*.

114. Poberevskii, "*Ocherk istorii Pravoslaviia v Amerike,*" 25.

115. Any of several marine and freshwater fishes of the family *Cottidae*.—Trans.

116. A kind of edible mushroom.—Trans.

117. In 1808, Father Herman was offered ordination to the priesthood.

118. *Amerikanskii Pravoslavnii Vestnik* [American Orthodox Messenger], 17 (1899): 469–70.

119. Now known as Sitka.—Trans.

120. *Amerikanskii Pravoslavnii Vestnik* [American Orthodox Messenger], 18: 492–93.

121. *Pis'mo S. I. Ianovskogo k igumenu Damaskinu ot 22 noiabria 1865 g.* [A letter of S. I Ianovskii to Hegumen Damascene of November 22, 1865], in *Valaamskie missioneri v Amerike (v kontse XVIII stoletiia)* [Valaam missionaries in America (in the end of the 18th century], (St Petersburg, 1900), 136.

122. Most likely, this passage concerns a document in which they asked Father Herman to teach in the school.

123. This refers to the voyage to New Al'bion (California) of the ship *Nicholas*, which was shipwrecked on November 1, 1808, to the north of the mouth of the Columbia River. The ship's crew was taken captive by Indians. In May 1810, the American Captain Brown from the ship *Lydia* ransomed thirteen people of the crew of the *Nicholas* from the Indians. By this time, seven people had died. One Creole, the boy Philip Kotel'nikov, the brother of Aleksei Kotel'nikov—one

of the best students in the Kodiak school—remained
forever in slavery to the Indians.

124. *Amerikanskii Pravoslavnii Vestnik* [American
Orthodox Messenger], 6 (1900), 126; also in the archives
of Spaso-Preobrazhenskii Valaamskii monastery, Op.
1/1/ Ed. Khr. 1, 1–4.

125. *Amerikanskii Pravoslavnii Vestnik* [American
Orthodox Messenger], 17 (1899), 467–69; also in
the archives of Spaso-Preobrazhenskii Valaamskii
monastery, Op. 1/1/ Ed. Khr. 1, 6–8.

126. *Valaamskie Podvizhniki* [Valaam ascetics] (St
Petersburg, 1997), 98.

127. *Pis'mo Petera, episkopa Novo-Arkhanrel'skogo,
vikariia Kamchatskoi eparkhii, ot 12 Maia 1866 g.* [A letter
of Peter, bishop of New Archangel, vicar of the Diocese
of Kamchatka of 12 May 1866], in *Valaamskie missioneri*
[Valaam Missionaries], 158.

128. S. Liashevskii, *Prepodobnyi starets German
Aliaskinskii* [The venerable elder Herman of Alaska]
(New York, 1952), 14.

129. *Appa* in Aleut literally means "grandfather" but
here is a title of respect, as with *elder.*—Trans.

130. Basil Michaelovich Golovnin, *Puteshestvie
na shliupe "Kamchatka" v 1817, 1818 I 1819 godakh*
[Travels on the sloop *Kamchatka* in 1817, 1818, and 1819]
(Moscow, 1965), 129.

131. *Zapiski kapitana 2-go ranga Golovnina o sostoianii
Aleutov v seleniiakh Rossiisko-Americanskoi kompanii, I o*

promyshlennikh eia [Notes of the captain of the second rank, Golovnin, about the condition of the Aleuts in the settlements of the Russian-American Company and about its *promyshlenniki*], in *Materiali dlia istorii russkikh zaselenii po beregam Vostochnogo okeana* [Materials for the history of the Russian settlements along the coasts of the eastern ocean], 1st ed. (St Petersburg, 1861), 117–18.

132. Ibid., 120–21.

133. Ibid., 119–20.

134. *Zapiski kapitana 2-go ranga Golovnina o nyneshnem sostoianii Rossiisko-Americanskoi kompanii (pisana v 1818 godu)* [Notes of the captain of the second rank, Golovnin, about the current condition of the Russian-American Company (written in 1818)], in *Materiali dlia istorii* [Materials for the history], 54.

135. *Valaamskie Podvizhniki* [Valaam ascetics], 103–5.

136. A. V. Grinev, *Pervye russkie poselentsy na Aliaske* [The first Russian settlers in Alaska] (Klio, 2001), 2: 52–65.

137. *Amerikanskii Pravoslavnii Vestnik* [American Orthodox Messenger], 17 (1899), 467.

138. Ibid.

139. *Pis'mo o. Germana k S. I. Ianovskomu ot 28 dekabria 1818 g.* [A letter of Father Herman to S. I. Ianovskii of December 28, 1818], in *Valaamskie missioneri* [Valaam missionaries], 151

140. *Batiushka* is a Russian term of endearment for a priest.

141. *Amerikanskii Pravoslavnii Vestnik* [American Orthodox Messenger], 18 (1899), 493–94.

142. *Pis'mo S. I. Ianovskogo* [A letter of S. I. Ianovskii], in *Valaamskie missioneri* [Valaam missionaries], 134–36.

143. Poberevskii, "*Ocherk istorii,*" 26.

144. *Pis'mo S. I. Ianovskogo* [A letter of S. I. Ianovskii], in *Valaamskie missioneri* [Valaam missionaries], 143–44.

145. *Istoriia Russkoi Ameriki (1732–1867), T. 2* [History of Russian America (1732–1867), Volume 2], 234–35.

146. The assertion of several historians that this event could not have happened because at this time there were no Jesuits in California but only Dominicans, should not be considered a serious argument. As is clear from Ianovskii's letter, he was told about this incident by the Kodiak Aleut Kykhliai, who knew neither Spanish nor Russian. Ianovskii was not concerned about which monastic order these Catholic monks belonged to. It is likely that he simply ascribed this event to the Jesuits, as a monastic order known for its inhuman treatment of Indians.

147. *Pis'mo S. I. Ianovskogo* [A letter of S. I. Ianovskii], in *Valaamskie missioneri* [Valaam missionaries], 136–37.

148. Ibid., 141.

149. Iu. Kholopov, *Odesseia leitenanta Ianovskogo: Zhizn' i prikliucheniia moreplavatelia, glavnogo pravitelia*

Russkoi Ameriki, kaluzhckogo dvorianina [The odyssey of Lieutenant Ianovskii: The life and adventures of the seafarer, chief manager of Russian America, and Kaluga nobleman] (Kaluga, 1998), 88.

150. 1 Cor 4:11.

151. Eph 6:12.

152. Eph 6:12.

153. One verst is 3,500 feet, or 0.6628 miles.

154. *Pis'mo o. Germana Valaamskomu igumenu Jonathanu ot 13 dekabria 1819 g.* [A letter of Father Herman to the Valaam Hegumen Jonathan of December 13, 1819], in *Valaamskie missioneri* [Valaam missionaries], 190–94.

155. Eph 6:12.

156. Matt 11:25.

157. *Pis'mo o. Germana k S. I. Ianovskomu ot 20 iiulia 1820 g.* [A letter of Father Herman to S. I. Ianovskii of July 20, 1820], in *Valaamskie missioneri* [Valaam missionaries], 145–48

158. Wrangell, "Kad'iakskii otdel, ostrov Kad'iak" [The Kodiak Department, Kodiak Island], in *Russkaia Amerika v neopublikovannykh* [Russian America, an unpublished manuscript], 244–45.

159. Liashevskii, *Prepodobnyi starets* [The venerable elder], 21–22.

160. *Pis'mo S. I. Ianovskogo* [A letter of S. I. Ianovskii], in *Valaamskie missioneri* [Valaam missionaries], 133–34.

161. *Amerikanskii Pravoslavnii Vestnik* [American Orthodox Messenger], 18 (1899), 494–95.

162. *Pis'mo M. I. Murav'ieva ķ o. Germanu ot 5 noiabria 1820 g.* [Letter of M. I. Murav'ev to Father Herman of November 5, 1820], Archives of the Russian-American Company, F. 62, No. 66, National Archives.

163. An old Russian measure, equivalent to 71 centimenters or approximately 28 inches; this makes 1.2 *arshin* equivalent to 85.2 centimeters or 33.5 inches.

164. *Pis'mo M. I. Murav'ieva ķ o. Germanu ot 5 noiabria 1820 g.* [Letter of M. I. Murav'ev to Father Herman of November 5, 1820], Archives of the Russian-American Company, F. 62, No. 68, National Archives.

165. *Amerikanskii Pravoslavnii Vestnik* [American Orthodox Messenger], 18 (1899), 497.

166. "*Rasskaz bogomol'tsa G. M. Lazareva ob o. Germane, oktiabr' 1864 g.*" [The story of the pilgrim G. M. Lazarev about Father Herman from October 1864], in *Valaamskie missioneri* [Valaam missionaries], 126.

167. *Svedeniia ob ottse Germane, cobrannye ot raznikh lits ķreolom K. Larionovym* [Information about Father Herman gathered from various people by the Creole K. Larionov], in *Valaamskie missioneri* [Valaam missionaries], 172–8.

168. A form of paper money used between 1769 and c. 1840.—Trans.

169. Poberevskii, *Ocherk istorii* [A sketch of the history], 28

170. L'vov, *Kratkie istorisheskie svedeniia* [Brief historical information about], 1370.

171. "*Rasskaz bogomol'tsa*" [The story of the pilgrim], in *Valaamskie missioneri* [Valaam missionaries], 125.

172. In ancient Greece, Cynics practiced a philosophy that held that the purpose of life is to live a life of virtue in agreement with nature. They rejected all conventional desires for wealth, fame, or power by living a simple life free from all possessions.

173. Wrangell, "*Kad'iakskii otdel, ostrov Kad'iak*" [The Kodiak Department, Kodiak Island], in *Russkaia Amerika v neopublikovannykh* [Russian America, an unpublished manuscript], 245.

174. Ibid.

175. One of the twelve great feasts of the Orthodox Christian Church year, the Meeting of the Lord marks the fortieth day after Christ's birth, when he was brought to the temple to be consecrated to God. The Righteous Simeon met Joseph, Mary, and her Child at the temple. According to tradition, Simeon had been waiting for 300 years to see the promised Savior of the Hebrews. Upon seeing the Christ Child, he said, "Lord, now You are letting Your servant depart in peace, according to Your word. For my eyes have seen Your salvation, which You have prepared before the face of all peoples, a light to bring revelation to the Gentiles, and the glory of Your people Israel" (Luke 2:29–32). Shortly thereafter he died.—Trans.

176. *Pis'mo I. Kupreianova k o. Germanu ot 3 marta 1836 g.* [Letter of I. Kupreianov to Father Herman

of March 3, 1836], Archives of the Russian-American
Company, F. 31, No. 47, National Archives.

177. *Pis'mo I. Kupreianova k o. Germanu ot 16
octiabria 1836 g.* [Letter of I. Kupreianov to Father
Herman of November 16, 1836], Archives of the Russian-
American Company, F. 351, No. 481, National Archives.

178. *Svedeniia ob ottse Germane, cobrannye ot
raznikh lits kreolom K. Larionovym* [Information about
Father Herman gathered from various people by the
Creole K. Larionov], in *Valaamskie Missioneri* [Valaam
missionaries], 175.

179. Ibid., 179.

180. Ibid., 181.

181. N. I. Ponomareva, *Prepodobnyj German
Aliaskinskii—pravoslavnyi apostol Ameriki* [Venerable
Herman of Alaska—Orthodox apostle to America],
http://elibrary.karelia.ru/book.shtml?id=546 also in
F. 341, On. 888, D. 1001, L. 142, *Arkhiv vneshnej politiki
Rossiiskoi imperii* [Archives of the foreign relations of the
Russian Empire].

182. For discussion of his actual age, see the
Introduction, p. xiii.

183. Ibid.

184. Peter Stepanovich Litvintsev (born 1813) was
the son of a priest. He graduated from the Irkutsk
Theological Seminary with honors; in 1838, he was
ordained a priest in Holy Trinity Church in Irkutsk and
assigned as a chaplain in the army. In 1840, by his own

free will, he was transferred to Kodiak. He was amazed at the decline of the local church: of 3,700 parishioners, more than 1,000 were not baptized and several hundred pairs were not married. From 1841 to 1843, Father Peter visited the settlements in his parish. *Iz putevogo zhurnala Kad'iakskogo Sviashchennika Petera Litvintseva* [From the travel journal of the Kodiak priest Peter Litvintsev], in *Khristianskoe chtenie* [Christian reading] (St Petersburg, 1845), ch. 1, 448–65.

In 1842, Father Peter blessed a new building for the church. In 1845, he was transferred to New Arkhangel'sk to be director of the theological seminary. In 1851, he was assigned dean of the American churches and in 1852 officially named rector of the seminary. In 1858, after eighteen years of missionary work in America, Father Peter left for Russia. In 1861, Archpriest Peter visited Blagoveshchensk in the retinue of Bishop Innocent, from where he departed for Nikolaevsk-on-the-Amur, where he was to serve.

185. M. V. Vinokurov, *Prep. German Aliaskinskii. O monastyre na ostrove Elovom i ob ubogom monakhe Germane* [Venerable Herman of Alaska. About the monastery on Spruce Island and about the wretched monk Herman], in *Russkii palomnik* [Russian pilgrim] (2004), 31: 184.

186. A form of paper money used between 1769 and c. 1840.—Trans.

187. Vinokurov, *Prep. German Aliaskinskii* [Venerable Herman].

188. Ibid., 185.

189. Il'ia Ivanovich Tyzhnov, *Putevoditel' Khristianina* [The guide of a Christian] (St Petersburg, 1847).

190. Il'ia Ivanovich Tyzhnov, *Aleutsko-kad'iakskii bukvar* [The Aleut-Kodiak dictionary] (St Petersburg, 1848).

191. Il'ia Ivanovich Tyzhnov, *Evangelie apostola Matfeia* [Gospel of the apostle Matthew] (St Petersburg, 1848).

192. Ivan Barsukov, *Innokentii mitropolit Moskovskii i Kolomenskii po ego sochineniiam, nis'mam i rasskazam sovremennikov* [Innocent, metropolitan of Moscow and Kolomensk, on the basis of his essays, letters, and contemporaries] (Moscow, 1883), 272.

193. Vinokurov, *Prep. German* [Venerable Herman], 186.

194. M. W. Falk, ed., *Holmberg's Ethnographic Sketches* (Fairbanks, 1985), 89.

195. *Zapiska ob o. Germane o. Petera Kashevarova ot 7 sentiabria 1866 g.* [Father Peter Kashevarov's notes about Father Herman of September 7, 1866], in *Valaamskie missioneri* [Valaam Missionaries], 186

196. The GPU was an earlier version of the KGB.—Trans.

197. *Svedeniia ob ottse Germane* [Information about father Herman], in *Valaamskie missioneri* [Valaam missionaries], 178.

198. *Kum* is a word used to address the father of one's godchild. It can also mean the godfather of one's child.

199. *Svedeniia ob ottse Germane* [Information about father Herman], in *Valaamskie missioneri* [Valaam missionaries], 175–6.

200. *Pis'mo igumena Damaskina k arkhiepiskopu Innokentiiu ot 27 dekabria 1866 g.* [Letter of Hegumen Damasken to Archbishop Innocent of December 27, 1866], in *Izbrannye trudy sviatitlia Innokentiia, mitropolita Moskovskogo i Kolomenskogo, apostola Siberi i Ameriki* [Selected works of bishop Innocent, metropolitan of Moscow and Kolomensk, apostle of Siberia and America] (Moscow, 1997), 350.

201. R. F. Pierce, *Russian America: A Biographical Dictionary* (Fairbanks, Alaska: Kingston, 1990), 166.

202. *Pis'mo S. I. Ianovskogo* [A letter of S. I. Ianovskii], in *Valaamskie missioneri* [Valaam missionaries], 144.

203. A *pannikhida* is a service for the departed.—Trans.

204. *Pis'mo arkhiepiskopa Innokentiia k igumenu Damaskinu ot 1 marta 1867 g.* [A letter of archbishop Innocent to hegumen Damaskene of March 1, 1867], in *Izbrannye trudy sviatitlia Innokentiia* [Selected works of bishop Innocent], 351.

205. *Iz putevogo zhurnala Innokentiia, episkopa Kamchatskogo, Kuril'skogo i Aleutskogo, vedennogo im vo vremia pervogo puteshestviia ego po vverennoi emu*

eparkhii v 1842 i 1843 godakh [From the travel diary of Innocent, bishop of Kamchatka, Kyril and Aleutian, kept by him during his first journey around the diocese which had been entrusted to him in 1842 and 1843], in *Izbrannye trudy sviatitlia Innokentii* [Selected works of bishop Innocent], 123–24.

206. *Spasaite detei. Poucheniia sviatitelia Innokentiia, mitropolita Moskovskogo, apostola Ameriki i Sibiri* [Save the children. The lessons of hierarch Innocent, metropolitan of Moscow, apostle of America and Siberia] (St Petersburg, 1997), 33–34.

207. *Svedeniia ob ottse Germane* [Information about father Herman], in *Valaamskie missioneri* [Valaam missionaries], 172.

208. *Zhizn' Valaamskago monakha Germana, amerikanskago missionera* [The life of the Valaam monk Herman, an American missionary], in *Strannik* [The wanderer] February (1868), 52–71; available in translation, along with other material, in *Little Russian Philokalia, Vol. III: St Herman*.

209. Father Stephen Liashevskii, *Neskol'ko slov ob avtope Akafista Prep. Germanu* [A few words about the author of the Akathist to St Herman], in *Russkii palomnik* [Russian pilgrim] (2000), 21–22: 59.

210. *Svedeniia ob ottse Germane* [Information about father Herman], in *Valaamskie missioneri* [Valaam missionaries], 177.

211. Liashevskii, *Neskol'ko slov* [A few words], in *Russkii palomnik* [Russian pilgrim], (2000), 21–2, 7.

212. The kamilavka is a circular, brimless hat with hard sides and a flat top. In Russian Orthodox monastic tradition, a monk wears a black kamilavka covered with a long black veil.

213. Sitka was called "New Arkhangel'sk" during Russian control of Alaska.

214. This was written in 2002.

215. *Pravoslavnaia Rus'*, 16 (1970).

216. The author of the article, Archimandrite Cyprian (Pizhov), here refers to himself.

217. 91st Cong., *Congressional Record* 116 (August 4, 1970), No. 133, p. 1.

218. Information taken from the work of the departed Rosa (Olga) Gavrilovna Liapunova, *Zapiski ieromonakha Gideona 1803–1807* [Notes of hieromonk Gideon 1803–1807], 1979, and one of the sources on the history and ethnography of Russian America, *Problemy istorii i etnografi Ameriki* [The problems of the history and ethnography of America] (Moscow: Nauka), 215–29. See also *Ocherki po istorii Amerikanskoi pravoslavnoi dukhovnoi missii* [Studies in the history of the American Orthodox spiritual mission] and Hieromonk Gideon, *The Round the World Voyage of Hieromonk Gideon, 1803–1809*. See also the posthumous edition of Liapunov's unfinished work, *Zapiski ieromonakha Gideona o*

Pervom russkom krugosvetnom puteshectbii I Russkoi Amerike [Notes of hieromonk Gideon about the first Russian round-the-world trip and Russian America], in *Russkaia Amerika: Po lichnim vpechatlenniiam missionerov, zemleprokhodtsev, moriakov, issledovatelei I drugikh ochevidtsev* [Russian America: By the personal impressions of missionaries, travelers, sailors, investigators and other witnesses], ed. A. D. Drudzo and R. V. Kizhalov (Moscow: Misl, 1994), 27–121. The letters of Father Gideon and information about St Herman are included in these publications.

219. Basil Michaelovich Golovnin, *Puteshestvie na shliupe "Kamchatka" v 1817, 1818 I 1819 godakh* [Travels on the sloop *Kamchatka* in 1817, 1818, and 1819] (Moscow, 1965), 129.

220. *Pis'mo S. I. Ianovskogo k igumenu Damaskinu ot 22 noiabria 1865 g.* [A letter of S. I Ianovskii to hegumen Damascene of November 22, 1865], in *Valaamskie missioneri v Amerike (v kontse XVIII stoletiia)* [Valaam missionaries in America (in the end of the eighteenth century)] (St Petersburg, 1900), 136.

221. Golovnin, *Puteshestvie na shliupe "Kamchatka"* [Travels on the sloop "Kamchatka"], 123–98.

222. Ibid., 184–86.

223. *Zapiski kapitana 2-go ranga Golovnina* [Notes of the captain of the second rank, Golovnin], in *Materiali dlia istorii russkikh zaselenii* [Materials for the history of the Russian settlements], 189

224. RAC document, departure papers, January 30, 1818, No. 36/38; error in numbering.

225. *Ocherki po istorii Amerikanskoi pravoslavnoi dukhovnoi missii* [Studies in the history of the American Orthodox spiritual mission] (Valaam Monastery, 1894) and Kholopov, *Odesseia leitenanta Ianovskogo* [The odyssey of lieutenant Ianovskii].

226. Ibid., Appendix.

227. These documents are located in RGIA, Archive 797, List 4, File 168466, p. 12 and the back.

INDEX

229